The Basic
ITALIAN COOKBOOK

The Basic

ITALIAN COOKBOOK

Compiled by **Lesley Pagett**

NEW HOLLAND

Contents

Introduction

If you think Italian food is only pizza, pasta and tomato sauce, then this cookbook will be a revelation. It's filled with fantastic food ideas from first course—antipasti—to decadent and delicious desserts. In between, you'll find recipes for vegetable dishes, and classic Italian main courses that feature seafood, poultry, lamb, beef and veal. There are also those traditional pasta and rice dishes that are easy to prepare and rich in flavour.

Italy is made up of 20 regions, including Piedmont and Lombardy in the north, Tuscany and Umbria in the centre, and Calabria, Sicily and Sardinia in the south. Each region has its own geographical and climatic characteristics varying from the mountainous north, which includes the beautiful Dolomite Alps, to the warm, coastal south with its vistas of rugged mountains, vast golden wheat fields, crystal clear seas, and age-old olive trees.

Over the centuries, each region developed its own political and social history, which in turn led to the development and refinement of certain cuisines. Each region produced its own recipes, relying on ingredients that were locally and regionally produced.

In Italy, there are often small variations of the same dish within the same region (for example, with pesto), but there are also distinctive variations. For example, although olive oil has become the standard condiment of Italian cuisine, butter is still more often used in the north than in the south of the country.

The regions are also renowned for specific produce. The most flavoursome sun-ripened tomatoes, olives, eggplants (aubergines) and capsicums (bell peppers) are mainly found in the south of Italy, while the finest hams traditionally come from the north. Pasta is more commonly eaten in the south, while polenta and bread are prolific in the north.

Despite all the variations, one thing that all Italians agree on is the pleasure of cooking and eating good food. Food is a passion in Italy, where even a modest meal can be magnificent, and it is around the dinner table that Italians love to gather to eat, drink, sing and discuss the merits of their food—all of which is rich, robust and rustic.

Italians regard freshness and quality as the most important aspects of preparing food. Italian cooks can turn the simplest and freshest ingredients into a feast, which is perfect for today's casual lifestyle and preference for a healthy diet. A simple pasta tossed with tomato sauce, or fish char-grilled and served with a dash of olive oil and a wedge of lemon are examples of this approach to simplicity.

Italian food offers choices for every palate and pocket. Traditionally, the main meal in Italy is lunch. With most shops, offices and schools closed between 1 and 4 pm, lunch in an Italian household is on the table any time from 1 pm onward. Lunch often comprises a first course of soup, rice or pasta, followed by a course of meat or fish, together with cheeses, vegetables or salad and, finally, fruit.

The evening meal, served any time after 8 pm, is usually a lighter version of lunch, with an emphasis on easily digestible foods, such as vegetables, salads, cheeses and fruit. Bread is part of every meal.

So bring Italy into your kitchen and celebrate the sun-drenched flavours, scents and colours of the Mediterranean.

Buon appetito!

The Ingredients

PASTA AND GNOCCHI

Pasta is considered the essence of Italian food. In Italy, pasta is an essential part of every full meal. Il primo, as pasta is called, is usually served between the antipasto and the main course.

Dried pasta is made from hard durum wheat and water, although it is sometimes enriched with eggs, giving it a lovely golden colour. It can also be coloured with spinach, to make it green, or squid ink to make it black. The elasticity in pasta dough makes it ideal for shaping into hundreds of different forms—such as long, thin strands called spaghetti, spirals (fusilli), bow tie shapes (farfalle) or shells (conchiglie). Fresh pasta is made from superfine flour, water and eggs, and is easily kneaded by hand. It is often wrapped around parcels of meat, vegetables and cheese to make ravioli, cannelloni, tortellini or cappeletti.

To cook pasta, fill a large pot with enough salted water to cover the pasta, and bring it to a brisk boil. Add a small amount of pasta at a time. If you are cooking spaghetti, hold it near the end and gently lower the strands into the boiling water; it gradually softens and curves around the pan as it enters the water. Boil pasta briskly, uncovered, stirring occasionally until just tender. The Italians call it al dente—which means the pasta should be firm when bitten between the teeth. Do not overcook. Drain in a colander, rinse with hot water, and stir through a dash of olive oil and salt (optional).

Gnocchi are small dumplings made from semolina, potatoes or flour. Gnocchi can be served as a first course accompanied by any pasta sauce, particularly a creamy Gorgonzola sauce or Bolognese sauce. Gnocchi are quite filling so usually only a small portion is eaten. The trick to cooking gnocchi is to only poach them in lightly salted, simmering water. They rise to the water's surface when ready.

RICE AND POLENTA

Rice and polenta are popular staples in Italian cooking and are usually eaten in the first course of a full Italian meal. Italian **rice** is classified by size, ranging from the shortest variety called *ordinario* (used in puddings) to *semifino* (used in soups and salads), *fino*, and the longer grains called *superfino* (used in risottos). Arborio rice is a type of superfino, and is known as the best rice for risottos. Rice should be cooked to a firm texture called *al dente*, which gives it a creamy smoothness while still retaining its shape.

Polenta has been a staple food in northern Italy for centuries. It is made from a grainy yellow flour from ground maize, which is cooked into a kind of porridge. Polenta can be quite coarse or very fine in texture and is very versatile. Although it is mainly served as a first course, it can be eaten with vegetables, during the main meal or made into cakes and biscuits.

MEAT AND POULTRY

Veal (*vitello*) is a favourite meat in Italy and is used in recipes from every region. Veal appears in hundreds of recipes, such as *veal scaloppine* and *veal parmigiano*. Veal can be served as cutlets, chops or a rolled roast. Lamb (*agnello*) is another popular meat eaten in Italy. It is cooked in a variety of ways from roasts to cutlets. Roast lamb is a traditional Easter dish. Pork (*maiale*) chops and cutlets are also enjoyed in Italy as well as beef (*manzo*). Chicken (*pollo*), pheasant (*fagiano*), quail (*quaglie*) and pigeon (*piccione*) are also eaten. Birds tend to be cooked slowly as a roast or in a casserole.

FISH AND SEAFOOD

The extensive water surrounding Italy's coast provides an abundance of fish and seafood. Popular fish include monkfish (*coda di rospo*), sole (*sogliola*), swordfish (*pesce spada*) sea bass (*spigola*) and red mullet (*triglia*).

The many rivers and lakes in Italy provide freshwater fish such as trout (*trota*), perch (*pesce persico*), carp (*carpione*) and eel (*anguilla*). Fish tend to be marinated with olive oil, lemon juice and herbs, baked or grilled, and served with vegetables.

Some varieties of fish are also dried, salted or preserved in oil. Tuna (*tonno*) is canned in olive oil, while anchovies (*acciughe*) and sardines (*sarde*) are salted and packed in oil.

Seafood is another staple of Italian cuisine, with calamari/squid (*calamari*), prawns/shrimp (*gamberetti*), vongole/clams (*vongole*), octopus (*polipi*) and mussels (*cozze*) featuring in many pasta, risotto and fish dishes.

CURED MEATS

Every region in Italy has its own distinct cured meats, with hundreds of different hams and salamis being produced commercially. Most cured meats are served as an antipasto before the main meal.

The most famous Italian cured meat is *prosciutto*. This thinly-sliced ham is salted and air-dried to create its rich, intense flavour. Prosciutto is often served with melon and figs, on slices of bread, rolled up with a thin slice of veal and sage, or chopped up and added to pasta. *Pancetta* is another commonly eaten cured meat that resembles unsmoked bacon. It is cured in salt and spices to give it a mild flavour.

There are dozens of salamis from Italy, all with a texture and flavour that reflects the region from which they hail. All salamis are made from pork, but vary according to the seasoning and fat used and the drying period of the meat. Salamis are commonly served as an antipasto, eaten with bread, or chopped up and added to pasta.

BREAD

Bread (*pane*) has always had a main role at the Italian table. No Italian meal is ever served without bread. Indeed, it often constitutes a meal in itself, such as bruschetta, crostini, or pizza. Today, thousands of bakeries (*panettieri*) prepare regional breads, differing in shape, taste, texture and ingredients. There are hundreds of different breads available and the texture and flavour depends on the type of flour used and the amount of seasoning added, but nearly all Italian breads are firm-textured with thick crusts.

Traditional Tuscan bread is made without salt, since it is designed to be eaten with cured meats such as salami and prosciutto. Southern Italian breads often contain olive oil, which goes well with tomatoes. Italians buy or make fresh bread every day. Any stale bread is made into breadcrumbs and used in soups, stuffings and salads.

CHEESE

Gorgonzola, pecorino, mascarpone, Parmesan, provolone, ricotta, mozzarella—the list of Italy's splendid cheeses (*formaggio*) is endless. Whether you're cooking with an Italian cheese, adding one to a cooked dish, or assembling a cheese platter, you're dealing with some of the world's best.

The cheeses of Italy originated in the dairies and kitchens of farmers. Now, each region has at least one cheese with which it is associated, and this is reflected in that region's cooking. What would a pizza be like without mozzarella, or a pasta dish without a grating of Parmesan? Many Italian cheeses are eaten at different stages of maturity, and are used as an accompaniment to a meal or eaten on their own after the main course.

Italian cheese can be divided into four categories: hard, semi-soft, soft and fresh. Hard cheeses include asiago, Parmesan, pecorino and provolone. Semi-soft cheeses include bel paese, fontina, taleggio and stracchino. Soft cheeses include Gorgonzola and caprini, and fresh cheeses include mascarpone, mozzarella and ricotta.

VEGETABLES

Italians almost always use fresh vegetables in season. Vegetables usually accompany meat, fish, soups, pasta or rice, or can be served as a dish on their own. The most common vegetables used in Italian cuisine are asparagus (*asparagi*), cardoons (*cardi*), artichokes (*carciofi*), cabbage (*cavolo*), onions (*cipolle*), fennel (*finocchio*), eggplants/ aubergines (*melazane*), capsicum/bell peppers (*peperoni*), spinach (*spinaci*), zucchini/ courgettes (*zucchini*), pumpkins and squash (*zucca*) and, of course, the humble tomato (*pomodori*).

Fresh salad leaves also feature. Italian salads tend to have a lot of flavour and texture due to the use of radicchio (*radicchio*), rocket/arugula (*rucola*), cornsalad (*valeriana*), and dandelion (*cicoria di campo*).

HERBS AND SEASONINGS

Herbs are vital to Italian cooking—their aromatic flavour adds depth to any dish. The use of rosemary and sage with meat, or basil with pasta and tomatoes creates unforgettable combinations.

Italians always use fresh herbs whenever possible. Dried herbs are stronger in flavour and often quite different in taste.

The most popular herbs in Italy are basil, marjoram, oregano, parsley, rosemary and sage. Basil is used in pesto and is found in many soups, salads and almost all tomato-based dishes. Marjoram is more commonly used in northern Italy to flavour meat, poultry, vegetables and soups. Oregano, which is related to marjoram and has a slightly stronger flavour, is used in southern Italy to flavour tomato dishes, vegetables and pizzas. Italian parsley is the flat-leaf variety, which has a more robust flavour than curly leaf parsley. It is used to flavour sauces, soups and risotto and also as a garnish.

Rosemary grows wild throughout Italy. It has an intense aroma, especially when dried. Rosemary goes well with roast veal, lamb, beef and chicken. A small sprig can enhance the flavour of fish and tomato dishes. It is also perfect with potatoes and onions. Sage also grows wildly in the Italian countryside. In northern Italy, sage is often used to flavour veal and chicken and vegetables.

ITALIAN WINE

The climate and soil of Italy are perfect for wine production and every region produces wine. Italian wines have a range of white and red varieties. White wines include Frascati, which is ideal with fish and chicken. It is a light wine that ranges from dry to sweet. Verdicchio is a light, fresh, fruity semi-dry wine.

Red wines include Lambrusco, which is a light, dry, slightly sparkling wine, that goes well with meat dishes. Barbera is a robust red wine which complements the full flavour of Italian food. Chianti is available either as red or white wine. As a young wine, it is wonderfully fragrant and fruity; as it ages it becomes even better. This is the wine that is found in the straw-covered bottles so often associated with Italy.

Marsala is a dessert wine named after a town on the island of Sicily. It is used mainly for cooking and dessert, however, some varieties are also drunk as aperitifs. Vin Santo is a dessert wine from Tuscany.

Asti Spumanti is the best-known sweet Italian sparkling wine that makes a perfect finish to a meal. It is made in huge quantities and exported all over the world.

BREAD and PIZZA

Mushroom Ciabatta

10 g (⅓ oz) dried porcini
   mushrooms
400 ml (14 fl oz) warm water
225 g (9 oz) fresh mushrooms,
   sliced
2 garlic cloves, crushed
2 tablespoons olive oil
450 g (1 lb) unbleached bread
   flour, plus extra for dusting
1 tablespoon salt
1 tablespoon granular yeast
cornmeal, for sprinkling

Makes 2 large oval loaves

Soak the mushrooms in warm water for at least 1 hour, then set them aside, and drain the liquid through a cheesecloth (muslin) two or three times to remove any grit and sand. Measure the liquid. Make up to 350 ml (12 fl oz) with additional water, if necessary. Pat the porcini dry, then roughly chop them.

Sauté the fresh mushrooms and garlic in 1 tablespoon of the oil over medium heat until soft, then raise the heat to high and simmer to reduce the mushroom liquid. Add the porcini to the mushroom mixture and set aside to cool.

In a pan, gently warm the porcini liquid.

Mix flour, salt and yeast together, then add half the mushroom mixture and warmed porcini water. Mix well with a wooden spoon, then turn out the dough out onto a lightly floured surface and knead thoroughly until soft and elastic.

Place the dough into an oiled bowl and cover with plastic wrap (cling film). Allow to rise for 2 hours, or until it has doubled in size.

Tip out the dough onto the work surface and divide in half. Shape each half into a flat oval, then scatter the mushroom mixture evenly each ovals and roll the dough up, tucking in the ends. Using your hands, flatten the loaves, then roll up again and shape into an oval. The loaves will be compact and quite small but they will rise quickly.

Place the loaves on an oven tray which has been sprinkled with cornmeal. Cover with a dampened tea towel and allow to rise for 2 hours or until doubled in size.

Preheat the oven to 200°C (400°F/Gas mark 6).

Brush the loaves with water, then bake for 40 minutes or until they are golden and crusty. Remove the loaves and cool on a wire rack.

Calzone

2 large pita breads

4 zucchini (courgettes), trimmed and cut into 4 cm (1½ in) chunks

2 red bell peppers (capsicums), seeds and pith removed and fruits halved

8–10 button (white) mushrooms, halved

olive oil, for brushing

1 tablespoon capers

2 tablespoons Sun-Dried Tomato Pesto (see page 275)

2 tablespoons Parmesan, grated (shredded)

Serves 4–6

Preheat the oven to 200°C (400°F/Gas mark 6).

Open the pita breads to make pockets.

Place the zucchini, capsicum (skin side up) and mushrooms on a baking tray and brush with oil. Grill (broil) until the zucchini are lightly golden and capsicum skins are blistered. Leave the capsicums to cool, then remove the skin, and thinly slice the flesh.

Place the vegetables in a bowl and mix in the capers and pesto. Carefully fill the pita bread with vegetable mixture. Brush the top of the pita bread with oil and sprinkle with Parmesan. Place on a baking sheet

Bake for 10 minutes, or until heated through. Serve warm cut into wedges.

Focaccia

1¼ teaspoons active dry
    yeast
1 teaspoon sugar
275 ml (10 fl oz) lukewarm
    water
1 tablespoon olive oil, plus
    extra for greasing and
    drizzling
450 g (1 lb) plain (all-
    purpose) flour, sifted,
    plus extra for dusting
coarse salt, for dusting

Makes 1

Place the yeast and sugar in a large bowl and stir in all but 1 tablespoon of the water. Cover and set aside in a warm place for 8–10 minutes, or until mixture is foaming.

Stir the remaining water and oil into the yeast mixture. Add one-third of the flour and stir until smooth. Stir in the another one-third of the flour, beat well, then add the remaining flour. Mix until a rough dough forms. Transfer to a floured surface and knead for 8–10 minutes, or until the dough is smooth and satin-like.

Place the dough in a lightly oiled bowl and roll around to coat the dough with oil. Cover the bowl tightly with plastic wrap (cling film). Set aside in a warm, draught-free spot for 1½ hours, or until the dough has doubled in size.

Knock back (punch down) the dough, then knead lightly and roll into the desired shape. Transfer to an oven tray lined with baking paper. Brush the surface with a little oil, cover with a clean kitchen towel and set aside to rise for another 30 minutes.

Using your fingertips, make dimple in the entire dough surface, pushing in about halfway. Cover again and set aside to rise for 1½–2 hours, or until doubled. Preheat the oven to 200°C (400°F/ Gas mark 6).

Drizzle the dough with olive oil and dust with coarse salt.

Bake for 15–20 minutes, or until golden brown. Sprinkle with additional oil if desired. Cut into squares and serve warm.

Note: Add other flavours, such as rosemary and sage, if you like. About 5 minutes before the end of cooking time, remove the bread from the oven, brush with olive oil and sprinkle with fresh herbs. Return to the oven for another 5 minutes, or until baked through.

Prosciutto Bread

2 tablespoons olive oil, plus
  extra for greasing
1 onion, thinly sliced
200 g (7 oz) prosciutto, finely
  chopped
340 g (12 oz/3 cups)
  unbleached strong bread
  flour, plus extra for dusting
1 tablespoon dried yeast
1 tablespoon fresh rosemary,
  chopped
1–2 teaspoons salt
  (depending on saltiness of
  prosciutto)
1 teaspoon sugar
55 g (2 oz) Parmesan, grated
  (shredded)
250 ml (8 fl oz/1 cup) warm
  milk
1 egg
1 egg yolk, beaten, for glazing

Makes 1 large loaf

In a frying pan, gently heat the olive oil. Add the onion and prosciutto to the pan and fry gently until the onion is translucent. Set aside to cool slightly.

In a large bowl, place the flour, yeast, rosemary, salt, sugar, 45 g/1½ oz) Parmesan, warm milk and egg. Add the onion mixture and mix well until combined, then tip the dough onto a floured surface. Knead for about 5 minutes, until the dough is smooth and elastic.

Place the dough in an oiled bowl, cover with cling film (plastic wrap) and set aside to rise in a warm place for 2 hours, or until doubled in size.

Turn out the dough onto a floured surface and knock back (punch down). Form into a ball and place on an oiled baking sheet. Cover as before and set aside to rise, until doubled in size.

Preheat the oven to 180°C (350°F/Gas mark 4).

Brush the bread with the egg yolk and sprinkle with the remaining Parmesan. Bake for 35 minutes or until cooked through, then leave to cool on a wire rack.

Spinach, Olive and Onion Bread

1 batch Focaccia dough (see
   recipe page 19)
1 tablespoon olive oil, for
   greasing
1 egg white, lightly beaten

FILLING
2 tablespoons olive oil
1 large red onion, sliced
1 garlic clove, crushed
1 tablespoon sultanas (golden
   raisins)
750 g (1 lb 10 oz) fresh
   spinach, stalks discarded
   and leaves shredded
125 g (4½ oz) stuffed green
   olives, sliced
3 tablespoons fresh
   mozzarella, grated
   (shredded)
freshly ground black pepper,
   to taste

Serves 8

Prepare the focaccia to the point where dough has doubled in size.

To make the filling, heat the olive oil in a large frying pan over gentle heat and fry the onion until soft. Add the garlic and sultanas and cook for 1 minute longer. Add the spinach and olives and cook until the spinach just begins to wilt. Remove from the heat and mix in the mozzarella. Season with black pepper. Set aside.

Preheat oven to 200°C (400°F/Gas mark 6).

Knock back (punch down) the dough and knead lightly. Divide the dough into four portions, and roll each out into 5 mm (¼ in) thick rounds. Place two rounds on baking sheets lined with baking paper, then spread the filling to within 2.5 cm (1 in) of the edge. Cover with the remaining rounds and pinch the sides together to seal the edges.

Brush the tops with olive oil. Cover with a kitchen towel and set aside to rise in a warm place until doubled in size.

Brush the top with egg white, and bake for 25 minutes, or until golden brown and well risen.

Tuscan Sage and Olive Bread

Sponge

225 g (8 oz) unbleached
 strong bread flour
2 tablespoons dried yeast
½ teaspoon salt
500 ml (17 fl oz/ 2 cups)
 lukewarm water

Dough

450 g (1 lb) unbleached strong
 bread flour, plus extra
100 g (3½ oz) large green
 stuffed olives, sliced
1 large bunch sage leaves,
 roughly torn
1 teaspoon salt
1 teaspoon freshly ground
 black pepper

Serves 4–6

To make the sponge, in a bowl, mix the flour with the yeast and
add the salt and water. Stir well to combine, cover and set aside
to rise in a warm place overnight.

The next morning, place 375 g (12½ oz) of the flour in a
large bowl. Make a well in the centre and add the sponge,
olives, sage, salt and pepper. Begin to mix all the ingredients,
incorporating extra flour as you go. Continue until the mixture
is very thick and difficult to stir. Tip out the dough onto a lightly
floured surface and knead for about 10 minutes until the dough
is smooth and elastic.

Divide the bread into two and shape each into an oval. Place
on a baking sheet and cover with cling film (plastic wrap). Allow
to rise until doubled in size.

Preheat the oven to 200°C (400°F/Gas mark 6).

Spray the dough with water just before baking. Bake for about
1 hour, spraying the bread with water every 10 minutes. Allow to
cool on a wire rack before serving.

Basil and Red Capsicum Pugliese

1.5 kg (3¼ lb) unbleached
   strong white bread flour,
   plus extra for dusting
1 tablespoon salt
1 teaspoon sugar
1 tablespoon dried yeast
1 bunch basil leaves, chopped
150 g (5 oz) roasted bell
   pepper (capsicum) pieces in
   oil, drained and chopped
140 ml (5 fl oz) olive oil, plus
   extra for greasing
900 ml (1½ pints/3¾ cups)
   lukewarm water

Makes 2 large loaves

Put the flour, salt, sugar and yeast into a very large bowl and stir briefly. Add the basil, capsicum, olive oil and water and mix until a dough forms. Add more water, if necessary.

Turn out the dough onto a well-floured surface and knead. You may need to divide the dough in half and knead each piece separately. Knead the dough for 10 minutes until it is soft, springy and satin-like—it should be slightly tacky but not overly sticky.

Place the dough into a very large, well-oiled bowl and cover with plastic wrap (cling film). Allow to rise in a cool, draught-free place until doubled in size, 2½–3 hours.

Turn the dough out onto a floured surface but do not knead. Divide the dough in half. Shape the loaves by placing them on an oiled baking sheet and pushing down the sides of the loaf and tucking them under the dough (almost like tucking sheets under a mattress). Do this to opposite sides of the dough at least eight times to create a tight surface over the loaf.

Preheat oven to 220°C (425°F/Gas mark 7).

Brush with water and allow to rise until doubled, about 1–1½ hours. Brush with water again and dust with flour. Bake for 45 minutes, or until the loaf sounds hollow when tapped underneath. Allow to cool on a wire rack.

Basic Pizza Dough

1½ teaspoons dry yeast
pinch of sugar
325 ml (10½ fl oz/1⅓ cups)
   warm water (about 41°C/
   105°F)
125 ml (4 fl oz/½ cup) olive oil
450 g (1 lb/4 cups) plain (all-
   purpose) flour, sifted, plus
   extra for dusting
1¼ teaspoons salt
olive oil, for greasing
cornmeal, for dusting

Makes 1 pizza base

In a small bowl, dissolve the yeast and sugar in the warm water and let stand for 5 minutes. Stir in the olive oil.

In a large bowl, combine the flour and salt. Add the yeast mixture and stir until the dough just holds together.

Turn the dough out onto a lightly floured surface and knead until smooth and silky, adding a little more flour if the dough seems sticky. Put the dough in an oiled bowl and turn to coat the surface. Cover the bowl with plastic wrap (cling film) and leave to rise in a warm place until doubled in size (about 1 hour).

Knock back (punch down) the dough using your fist in a straight-down motion.

Tip out onto a lightly floured surface, and roll to shape. Place on a baker's peel or oiled pizza pan dusted with cornmeal. Any excess dough can be wrapped in plastic wrap (cling film) and refrigerated.

NOTE: A simple, straightforward dough enriched with oil, this one is ready to use in a little more than an hour. For a firm, elastic dough that yields a crisp, finely textured crust, replace up to half the flour with semolina, a high-protein flour ground from hard durum wheat.

Original Tomato Pizza

2 quantities Basic Pizza
   Dough (see recipe page 24)
olive oil
5 ripe tomatoes, sliced
4 garlic cloves, sliced
handful fresh oregano leaves,
   chopped
freshly ground black pepper

Makes 2

Preheat the oven to 400°F/200°C/Gas mark 6.

Divide the dough into two portions and shape each into a 30 cm (12 in) round. Place the rounds on lightly greased baking sheets and brush with oil.

Arrange half the tomato slices, garlic and oregano on top of each pizza base and season to taste with black pepper. Bake for 15–20 minutes, or until crisp and golden.

Artichoke Pizza

225 g (8 oz) wholemeal
   (whole-wheat) self-raising
   (self-rising) flour
85 g (3 oz) butter
½ teaspoon salt
olive oil
1 tablespoon tomato purée
200 g (7 oz) can artichoke
   hearts, drained and halved
2 medium tomatoes, skinned
   and sliced
1 teaspoon dried oregano
115 g (4 oz) Cheddar cheese,
   finely sliced
12 black olives, pitted and
   halved

Makes 1

Preheat the oven to 375°F/190°/Gas mark 5. Mix the flour, butter and salt together in a large bowl and add enough warm water to make a pliable dough.

Roll out the dough into a 10 in (25 cm) round and place on a greased baking tray (sheet).

Brush with olive oil and spread with tomato purée. Arrange the artichokes and tomatoes on top and scatter with oregano.

Arrange the cheese over the tomatoes and place the olives on top.

Bake for about 35 minutes.

Cheese, Tomato and Onion Pizza

1 lb (450 g) wholemeal
  (whole-wheat) flour
7 g/¼ oz sachet dried yeast
1 teaspoon ground coriander
1 teaspoon sea salt
1 teaspoon ground caraway
  seeds
2 eggs
150 ml (¼ pint/⅔ cup)
  lukewarm milk
75 g (2½ oz) butter, melted
  then cooled, plus extra for
  greasing

Topping
30 g (1 oz) butter
400 g (14 oz) Roma tomatoes,
  sliced
200 g (7 oz) onions, finely
  chopped
4 fresh chillies, deseeded and
  sliced
200 g (7 oz) Emmental
  cheese, grated (shredded)
4 tablespoons Parmesan
2–3 teaspoons caraway seeds

Makes 1

For the dough, sift the flour into a mixing bowl and mix in the dried yeast, ground coriander, salt, ground caraway seeds, eggs, milk and butter. Knead to form a smooth dough, then cover and set aside in a warm place until risen and doubled in size. Knead the dough again, then roll out onto a greased baking tray. Set aside.

For the topping, melt the butter in a frying pan, add the onions and cook until softened. Set aside to cool.

Preheat the oven to 200°C/ 400°F/Gas mark 6.

When cool, arrange the onions, tomatoes, chillies and cheese on the pizza base, then sprinkle with caraway seeds.

Bake for about 20–25 minutes. Serve hot.

Pizza Supremo

2 quantities Basic Pizza
  Dough (see recipe page 24)
oil, for greasing
150 g (5 oz/¾ cup) tomato
  paste (purée)
1 green bell pepper
  (capsicum), chopped
150 g (5 oz) pepperoni or
  salami, sliced
150 g (5 oz) ham or prosciutto,
  sliced
115 g (4 oz) mushrooms,
  sliced
400 g (14 oz) can pineapple
  pieces, drained
55 g (2 oz) pitted olives
115 g (4 oz) mozzarella
  cheese, grated (shredded)
115 g (4 oz) mature Cheddar
  cheese, grated (shredded)

Makes 2

Preheat the oven to 400°F/200°C/Gas mark 6.

Prepare the pizza dough. Divide the dough into two portions and shape each to form a 30 cm (12 in) round. Place each on greased baking trays and spread with tomato paste.

Arrange half the green capsicum, pepperoni or salami, ham or prosciutto, mushrooms, pineapple and olives attractively on each pizza base.

Combine the cheeses and scatter half the mixture over each pizza. Bake for 25–30 minutes or until the cheese is golden and the base is crisp.

Pepperoni Pizza

2 quantities Basic Pizza
  Dough (see recipe page 24)
oil, for greasing
150 g (6 oz/²/₃ cup) tomato
  paste (purée)
200 g (7 oz) button (white)
  mushrooms, sliced
1 green bell pepper
  (capsicum), chopped
20 slices pepperoni
20 slices cabanossi (or salami)
  sausage
225 g (8 oz) mozzarella
  cheese, grated (shredded)

Makes 2

Preheat the oven to 200°C/400°F/Gas mark 6.

Prepare the pizza dough, then shape it into two 30 cm (12 in) rounds and place on greased baking trays (sheets).

Spread each round with tomato paste, then top each base with half the mushrooms and capsicum.

Arrange half the pepperoni and cabanossi sausage on each pizza and scatter each half with mozzarella.

Bake for 25–30 minutes, or until cheese is golden and base is crisp.

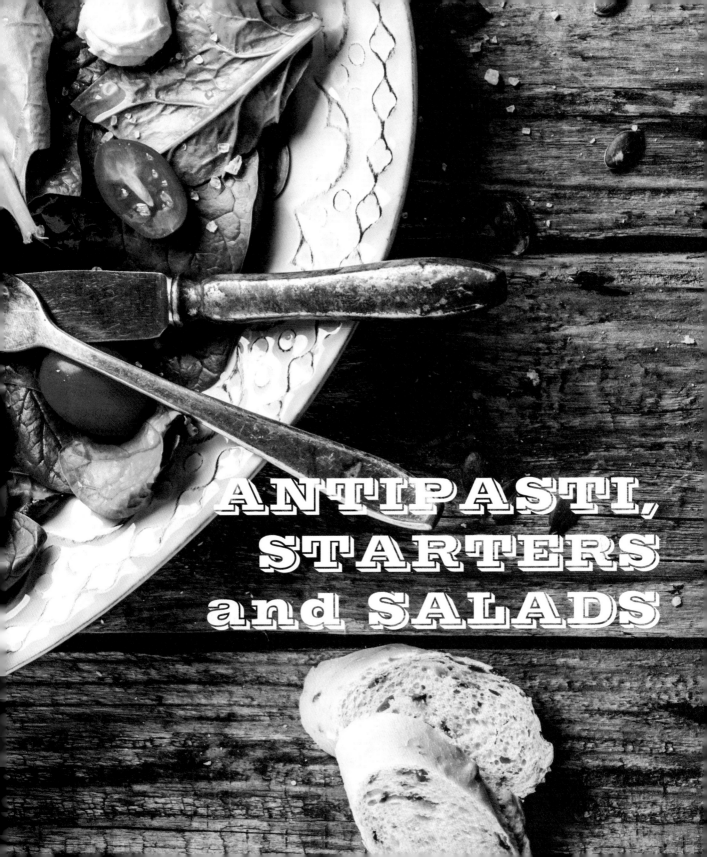

ANTIPASTI, STARTERS and SALADS

Roast Capsicum in Garlic

3 red bell peppers
    (capsicums), each cut
    lengthwise into eight
1½ tablespoons olive oil
5 garlic cloves, finely chopped
1 fresh red chilli, finely sliced
½ teaspoon dried oregano

Serves 6

Preheat the oven to 180°C (350°F/Gas mark 4).

Put the red capsicum in a bowl. In a separate bowl, combine the oil, garlic, red chilli and oregano. Pour over the capsicum and toss to coat.

Arrange the capsicum, skin side up, in a baking dish, cover with aluminium foil and bake for 30 minutes. Uncover and bake for 20–30 minutes longer, or until the capsicum blackens slightly.

Note: When available, use a mixture of red, green and yellow capsicums. Store, covered with olive oil, in a clean glass jar for up to 3 weeks. The capsicums taste best served at room temperature.

Bruschetta with Bocconcini and Basil

1 ciabatta loaf or French
  baguette, cut into 2 cm
  (¾ in) slices
60 ml (2 fl oz/¼ cup) olive oil
45 g (1½ oz) sun-dried tomato
  paste
175 g (6 oz) bocconcini, each
  ball cut into 5 slices
30 g (1 oz) fresh basil leaves,
  chopped or whole

Serves 6

Grill (broil) the bread slices for 2–3 minutes on each side. Brush each slice with olive oil, spread with a little sun-dried tomato paste and top with bocconcini slices and basil.

Bruschetta with Tomato and Basil

1 ciabatta loaf or French
  baguette, cut into 2 cm
  (¾ in) slices
olive oil, for brushing
2 garlic cloves, roasted and
  crushed
400 g (14 oz) Roma tomatoes,
  diced
1 small red onion, finely
  chopped
1 tablespoon fresh basil,
  chopped
1 tablespoon balsamic vinegar
2 tablespoons olive oil
salt and freshly ground black
  pepper, to taste

Serves 4–6

Grill (broil) the bread slices for 2–3 minutes on each side. Brush each slice with a little olive oil and spread a thin layer of roasted garlic on each slice.

In a bowl, mix together the tomatoes, onion, basil, vinegar and olive oil and season with salt and pepper.

Serve the toast with the tomato mixture piled on top.

Vegetable Toasts

2 courgettes (zucchini), thinly
sliced lengthwise
2 carrots, thinly sliced
lengthwise
2 red bell peppers
(capsicums), thinly sliced
sea salt and freshly ground
black pepper
4 thick slices white bread
1 tablespoon sunflower oil

Dressing
2 tomatoes
4 tablespoons extra virgin
olive oil
2 scallions (spring onions),
sliced
1 tablespoon white wine
vinegar

Serves 4

Place the courgette, carrots and bell peppers in a bowl and season well. (If you like you can use a vegetable peeler to make long ribbons with the courgette and carrots.)

Heat the sunflower oil in a large frying pan over a high heat and cook the vegetables for 4 minutes, stirring all the time, until they have softened and are just tender. Remove and set aside.

Meanwhile, toast the bread for 3 minutes each side, or until golden brown.

For the dressing, to skin the tomatoes, slice a cross in the base of each tomato. Put the tomatoes in a bowl of boiling water for 30 seconds, remove with a slotted spoon and when cool enough to handle, discard the peel and seeds, and finely chop the flesh.

Heat the olive oil in a pan and add the scallions and white wine vinegar. Cook, stirring occasionally, for 1–2 minutes until hot, then stir in the tomatoes. Pile the vegetables on top of the toast slices, drizzle with the hot tomato dressing and serve.

Crumbed Calamari

750 g (1¾ lb) squid tubes
  (squid hoods)
olive oil, for deep frying

Batter
55 g (2 oz) plain (all-purpose)
  flour
55 g (2 oz) cornflour (corn
  starch)
1 teaspoon baking powder
salt and freshly ground black
  pepper
250 ml (8 fl oz/1 cup) cold
  water

Serves 6

Cut squid tubes into 5 mm (¼ inch) rings. Place rings on paper towels and dry well.

Sift plain flour, cornflour and baking powder into a bowl. Add salt and pepper. Gradually add water and beat lightly—it doesn't matter if the flour remains slightly lumpy.

Heat oil to smoking point (it may spit and splatter, so be careful). Dip squid rings into batter, allow to drain slightly, and place in oil.

Cook until lightly golden (3 minutes maximum). Drain well and serve hot with tartare sauce or seafood sauce.

Marinated Calamari with Lemon and Herb Dressing

⅓ cup (2¾ fl oz) lemon juice
3 garlic cloves, crushed
125 ml (4 fl oz/½ cup) olive oil
1 kg (2 lb) calamari (squid), cut
   into thin rings

Dressing
¼ cup (2 fl oz) lemon juice
⅓ cup (2¾ fl oz) olive oil
1½ tablespoons fresh parsley,
   chopped
1 garlic clove, crushed
1 teaspoon Dijon mustard
salt and freshly ground black
   pepper, to taste

Serves 4–6

Combine lemon juice, garlic and oil in a bowl. Add calamari and marinate for at least 3 hours. If time permits, marinate overnight.

To make the Dressing, place all ingredients in a bowl and whisk well until dressing thickens slightly.

Heat a little oil in a pan, add calamari, and cook for a few minutes, until calamari is cooked through. Alternatively, the calamari can be cooked on a char-grill plate.

Serve calamari with lemon and herb dressing drizzled over.

Beef Carpaccio

450 g (1 lb) cooked beef fillet,
  sliced into 5 mm (¼ in)
  slices
115 g (4 oz) rocket (arugula),
  washed
1 tablespoon balsamic vinegar
3 tablespoons extra virgin
  olive oil, plus extra for
  greasing
pecorino cheese, shaved
salt and freshly ground black
  pepper, to taste

Serves 6

Lightly oil a sheet of baking paper and season it lightly with salt and freshly ground black pepper. Arrange four slices of beef on the baking paper approximately 5 cm (2 in) apart. Place another oiled piece of baking paper on top, and gently beat the meat, until it has spread out to at least twice its size. Repeat with the remaining meat slices. Refrigerate until needed.

Place the rocket in the centre of a serving plate, arrange the beef slices on top, and drizzle with balsamic vinegar and olive oil. Serve with shavings of pecorino cheese, and season with black pepper and salt.

Smoked Salmon Carpaccio with Extra Virgin Olive Oil and Lemon

(2 fl oz/ ¼ cup) extra virgin
   olive oil

3 tablespoons lemon juice

1 small red (Spanish) onion,
   finely chopped

2 teaspoons small whole
   capers

340 g (12 oz) smoked salmon,
   allow 3–4 slices per person

1 tablespoon fresh parsley,
   roughly chopped

freshly ground black pepper,
   to taste

capers, extra, to garnish

Serves 4

Combine oil, lemon juice, onion and capers in a bowl, and whisk.
   Arrange smoked salmon on serving plates.
   Drizzle dressing over smoked salmon, sprinkle with parsley
and pepper, and serve. Garnish with extra capers.

Red Capsicum and Potato Frittata

4 eggs

salt and freshly ground black
  pepper, to taste

2 potatoes, peeled and grated

1 zucchini (courgette), ends
  removed and grated

2 red bell peppers
  (capsicums), roasted, cut
  into thin strips

3 tablespoons olive oil

Makes 16 wedges

In a bowl, lightly beat eggs. Season with salt and pepper. Mix in potatoes, zucchini and capsicums.

Heat oil in a large frying pan. Pour in egg mixture and cook over medium heat for 8 minutes or until egg is set. Cut in half, turn and cook other side until golden.

To serve, cut into 16 small wedges. Serve warm or cold.

Roast Pumpkin, Potato and Rosemary Frittata

280 g (10 oz) butternut
   pumpkin, peeled, seeded
   and diced into 2 cm (¾ in)
   pieces
200 g (7 oz) potatoes, peeled
   and diced into 2 cm (¾ in)
   pieces
200 g (7 oz) sweet potato,
   peeled and diced into 2 cm
   (¾ in) pieces
1 tablespoon olive oil
2 sprigs rosemary, roughly
   chopped
4 eggs
125 ml (4 fl oz/½ cup) single
   (light) cream
125 ml (4 fl oz/½ cup) milk
1 garlic clove, crushed
55 g (2 oz) Parmesan, grated
salt and freshly ground black
   pepper, to taste

Makes 12

Preheat the oven to 220°C (425°F/Gas mark 7).

Place the pumpkin, potato, sweet potato, oil, 1 sprig of rosemary and a pinch of sea salt in a baking dish. Mix together and bake for 20 minutes, or until just cooked.

Grease and line a 12-cup muffin tin (pan) with baking paper.

In a bowl, mix together the eggs, cream, milk, garlic, cheese, remaining rosemary, salt and pepper. Add the potato, pumpkin and sweet potato.

Divide equally between the muffin cups, reduce the oven temperature to 180°C (350°F/Gas mark 4) and bake for 30–35 minutes. Serve hot.

Artichoke Salad with Pesto Dressing

bunch watercress, washed
400 g (14 oz) can artichoke
  hearts, drained
4 tomatoes, peeled and diced
2 bocconcini cheese, sliced

Pesto Dressing

55 g (2 oz) fresh basil leaves
2 tablespoons olive oil
1 garlic clove, crushed
3 tablespoons Parmesan,
  grated
2 tablespoons pine nuts,
  toasted

Serves 4

Break the watercress into small pieces and place in a salad bowl. Arrange the artichoke hearts, tomatoes and bocconcini cheese over the watercress.

To make the Pesto Dressing, place the basil, oil, garlic, Parmesan and pine nuts in a food processor or blender and process until smooth. Drizzle over the salad and toss gently to coat the salad ingredients.

Baby Spinach, Toasted Pine Nuts and Avocado Salad

80 g (2²/₃ oz) coppa, sliced
200 g (7 oz) baby spinach
55 g (2 oz) pine nuts, toasted
1 avocado, sliced
60 ml (2 fl oz/¼ cup) olive oil
2 tablespoons balsamic
   vinegar
30 g (1 oz/¼ cup) pecorino
   shavings
salt and freshly ground black
   pepper, to taste

Serves 4–6

Place the slices of coppa under a hot grill (broiler) and grill (broil) until crispy. Place the coppa, spinach, pine nuts and avocado in a bowl.

Mix together the oil and balsamic vinegar in a small bowl, pour over the salad, then toss through the pecorino shavings. Season with salt and pepper and serve.

Italian Tuna and Bean Salad

200 g (7 oz) can tuna in oil,
   drained and oil reserved
400 g (14 oz) can borlotti
   beans, drained and rinsed
1 small red onion, thinly sliced
2 sticks celery, thinly sliced
3 tablespoons fresh flat-leaf
   parsley, chopped

DRESSING
4 tablespoons olive oil
2 tablespoons balsamic or
   white wine vinegar
salt and freshly ground black
   pepper

Serves 4

To make the dressing, whisk the reserved tuna oil with the olive oil and vinegar, then season.

Flake the tuna into a large bowl and mix with the borlotti beans, red onion, celery and parsley. Spoon over the dressing and toss well to combine.

Note: The combination of colours, flavours and textures in this simple salad has made it a real favourite in Italy. It's delicious served with some warmed ciabatta bread.

Tuscan White Beans

250 ml (8 fl oz/1 cup) extra
  virgin olive oil
2 garlic cloves, peeled and
  sliced
1 red chilli, sliced lengthwise
5 sage leaves, finely sliced
zest and juice of 1 lemon
400 g (14 oz) cannellini beans,
  drained and rinsed
30 g (1 oz) parsley, chopped
salt and white pepper
1 onion, finely diced
1 stalk celery, finely sliced
1 carrot, peeled and finely
  diced

Serves 4

Heat half of the oil in a medium pan set over moderate heat. Add the garlic and cook gently. Add the chilli, half of the sage and half of the lemon juice and simmer very slowly for 15 minutes. Remove the chilli and add 2 tablespoons of cannellini beans and mash them through the oil.

Add the parsley, season to taste, stir and remove from the heat.

Combine the remaining ingredients, pour over the dressing and season to taste.

Stand for 15 minutes before serving.

Fennel and Orange Salad

1 bunch curly endive (frisée),
   leaves separated and
   washed
1 small fennel bulb, cut into
   thin strips
3 oranges, peeled and
   segmented
1 onion, sliced
20 black olives

Orange Dressing

3½ tablespoons olive oil
3 tablespoons white wine
   vinegar
1 tablespoon fresh fennel
   leaves, chopped
½ teaspoon orange zest,
   grated (shredded)
½ teaspoon sugar
freshly ground black pepper,
   to taste

Serves 6

Place the endive on a large serving platter. Arrange fennel, oranges, onion and olives on top.

To make the Orange Dressing, place the oil, vinegar, fennel, zest, sugar and black pepper in a screw-top jar. Shake well to combine. Pour the dressing over the salad and serve immediately.

Pasta Salad

450 g (1 lb) spiral (fusilli) pasta
1 tablespoon olive oil
½ teaspoon salt
½ red bell pepper (capsicum),
    seeds and pith removed,
    and flesh diced
4–6 button (white)
    mushrooms, sliced
4–6 shallots, finely chopped
115 g (4 oz) mung beans
115 g (4 oz) sweet corn
    kernels (optional)
300 ml (½ pint) salad dressing

Serves 6–8

Put the pasta into a large pan of boiling water with the oil and salt, and cook for 8 minutes, or until *al dente*. Rinse and strain.

Place all the ingredients except for the dressing in a bowl and toss to combine. Add the dressing to taste.

Mediterranean Chicken Pasta Salad

200 g (7 oz) spiral (fusilli) pasta

100 g (3½ oz) basil pesto

200 g (7 oz) sun-dried
  tomatoes in oil, sliced

200 g (7 oz) snow peas
  (mangetout), blanched and
  sliced

10 small mushrooms, sliced

1 stick of celery, sliced

1.5 kg (3¼ lb) cold cooked
  chicken, cut into bite-sized
  pieces

2 tablespoons balsamic
  vinegar

salt and freshly ground black
  pepper, to taste

1 lettuce, washed and leaves
  torn

Serves 6

Place the pasta in a large pan and cover with salted water. Bring to the boil and cook until *al dente*, about 8 minutes. Rinse in cool water and drain.

While the pasta is still warm, tip into a bowl and stir in the pesto and sun-dried tomatoes in their oil.

Stir the snow peas, mushrooms and celery into the pasta, then add the cooked chicken. Sprinkle over the balsamic vinegar and stir in, then season with salt and pepper. Refrigerate for a few hours, if possible, before serving.

To serve, put a layer of lettuce leaves on each plate, then top with chicken and pasta mix.

Insalata Caprese

400 g (14 oz) Roma tomatoes,
thickly sliced
250 g (9 oz) bocconcini, sliced
15 g (½ oz) fresh basil leaves
Crusty bread, to serve

Dressing
4 tablespoons extra-virgin
olive oil
2 tablespoons balsamic
vinegar
salt and freshly ground black
pepper

Serves 4

Arrange the tomatoes, bocconcini and basil leaves on individual plates.

Drizzle with olive oil and balsamic vinegar, and sprinkle with salt and freshly ground black pepper.

Serve with crusty bread.

Raddichio Anchovy Salad

1 radicchio lettuce, washed
  and leaves separated
½ bunch curly endive
  (frisée), washed and leaves
  separated
1 chicory, washed and leaves
  separated
8 radishes, washed and sliced
3 tablespoons fresh Italian flat-
  leaf parsley, chopped

Dressing
60 ml (2 fl oz/¼ cup) olive oil
60 ml (2 fl oz/¼ cup) lemon
  juice
60 ml (2 fl oz/¼ cup) dry white
  wine
3 anchovy fillets, drained and
  chopped
2 garlic cloves, crushed
½ teaspoon sugar

Serves 6

Arrange radicchio, endive and chicory attractively on a large platter. Top with radishes and parsley.

To make the dressing, place the oil, lemon juice, wine, anchovies, garlic and sugar in a food processor or blender and process until smooth.

Drizzle the dressing over the salad just before serving.

Roasted Tomatoes and Bell Pepper Salad

1 tablespoon olive oil

1 teaspoon oregano, chopped

½ teaspoon sugar

freshly ground black pepper

2 Roma tomatoes, cut into
   quarters and semi-roasted

1 red bell pepper (capsicum),
   halved

½ bunch rocket (arugula)

30 g (1 oz) pine nuts, roasted

2 hard-boiled eggs, quartered

25 g (¾ oz) spring onions
   (scallions), sliced

Dressing

60 ml (2 fl oz/¼ cup) olive oil

1 tablespoon balsamic vinegar

2 teaspoons sesame oil

½ teaspoon sugar

Serves 4

Preheat oven to 120°C (250°F/Gas mark 1).

Combine the olive oil, oregano and sugar in a bowl. Season with pepper and brush over the tomatoes.

Place the tomatoes and capsicum (skin side up) on a baking sheet and bake for 1 hour.

Place the rocket, pine nuts, eggs and spring onions in a bowl. Add the tomatoes and bell pepper.

Combine the dressing ingredients, and pour over the salad before serving.

Asparagus with Pecorino and Pancetta

450 g (1 lb) asparagus
juice of 1 lemon
100 ml (3½ fl oz) extra virgin
  olive oil
salt and freshly ground black
  pepper, to taste
8 thin slices pancetta, cut into
  pieces
75 g (2½ oz/1 cup) pecorino,
  shaved

Serves 4–6

Trim and discard the thick asparagus ends. Cook the asparagus in boiling water for 4 minutes, until slightly tender. Run under cold water until cool, then dry on paper towels.

To make the dressing, place the lemon juice in a bowl and slowly add the oil, whisking until thick. Season with salt and pepper.

Pour the dressing over the asparagus and serve with pancetta and pecorino cheese shavings.

Spicy Asparagus with Pine Nuts

450 g (1 lb) fresh asparagus
   spears, trimmed and cut
   into 5 cm (2 in) pieces
15 g (½ oz) butter
55 g (2 oz) pine nuts
115 g (4 oz) spicy Italian
   salami, cut into 5 mm (¼ in)
   cubes
2 tablespoons fresh basil,
   chopped
3 tablespoons fresh
   Parmesan, grated
   (shredded)

Serves 4

Steam the asparagus until just tender, about 3–4 minutes. Drain and rinse under cold running water to refresh, then drain again and set aside.

Heat the butter in a frying pan and fry the pine nuts and salami until lightly browned. Add the asparagus and basil and cook, for 1 minute, or until heated through, stirring constantly.

Scatter over the Parmesan and serve immediately.

Note: Use bacon instead of salami for a less spicy flavour.

Aubergine Antipasto

2 eggplants (aubergines), cut
    into 2 cm (¾ in) slices
salt
olive oil
150 g (5 oz) mozzarella
    cheese, sliced
1 tablespoon capers
2 gherkins, sliced lengthwise
2 tomatoes, sliced
12 slices ham or prosciutto,
    rolled
4 lettuce leaves
4 tablespoons chutney or
    relish
4 slices rye or wholemeal
    (whole-wheat) bread

Serves 4

Sprinkle the eggplant slices with salt, then set aside for 15–20 minutes to help draw out the bitter juices. Rinse under cold water and pat dry with paper towels.

Brush the eggplant lightly with olive oil. Place under a preheated grill (broiler) for 4–5 minutes each side, or until cooked through.

In a shallow baking dish, arrange the eggplant so that the slices overlap. Top with mozzarella and grill (broil) for 4–5 minutes, or until the cheese melts.

Divide the eggplant between four plates. Top with a few capers and serve with gherkins, tomatoes, ham, bread, lettuce and chutney. Serve with rye bread.

Note: Salting before cooking also stops large quantities of oil being soaked up by the eggplant.

Aubergine, Bell Pepper, Tomato and Bocconcini with Balsamic Dressing

60 ml (2 fl oz/¼ cup) olive oil

2 large eggplants (aubergine), cut into 8 slices, each 1–1.5 cm (½–¾ in) thick

1 red bell pepper (capsicum), quartered, seeded, roasted and finely sliced

4 Roma tomatoes, cut into 1 cm (½ in) slices and roasted

4 bocconcini balls, each cut into 3 slices

fresh basil leaves, to garnish

freshly ground black pepper, to taste

crusty Italian bread, to serve

Balsamic Dressing

60 ml (2 fl oz/¼ cup) olive oil

2 tablespoons balsamic vinegar

salt and freshly ground black pepper, to taste

Serves 4

Preheat the oven to 150°C (300°F/Gas mark 2).

Heat a char-grill pan and brush lightly with oil. Brush the eggplant slices with oil and char-grill for 2–3 minutes each side. Place the bell pepper under a hot grill (broiler), and cook until the skin blisters.

Brush the tomato slices with oil, season with pepper, place on a lightly oiled baking sheet, and roast in the oven for 20–30 minutes.

On each serving plate, place 2 slices of eggplant, top with 3 strips of bell pepper, 3 tomato slices, and 3 slices bocconcini. Garnish with basil leaves.

To make the dressing, combine all the ingredients. Drizzle over the dish, and season with salt and black pepper just before serving.

Serve with crusty Italian bread.

SOUPS

Crab Bisque

225 g (8 oz) can fresh or
   crabmeat
55 g (2 oz) butter
4 tablespoons plain (all-
   purpose) flour
1.25 litres (2 pints) milk,
   scalded
pinch of freshly grated nutmeg
salt and freshly ground black
   pepper, to taste
4 tablespoons dry sherry
whipped cream, to garnish
paprika, to garnish

Serves 6

Flake the crabmeat and pass it through a food processor or blender.

Make a roux by melting the butter in a pan over medium heat, and blending in the flour until smooth. Cook for 2–3 minutes. Add the milk and stir continuously until thick and smooth. Add the nutmeg and season with salt and pepper. Cook gently for 12–15 minutes. Add the prepared crabmeat and continue cooking for another 5 minutes. Just before serving, stir in the sherry.

Serve hot or cold, topped with a spoonful of whipped cream and sprinkled with paprika.

Cream of Mushroom Soup

225 g (8 oz) mushrooms
115 g (4 oz) butter
salt and freshly ground black
  pepper, to taste
3 garlic cloves, finely chopped
1.25 litres (2 pints) chicken
  stock
125 ml (4 fl oz/½ cup) single
  (light) cream, at room
  temperature
French bread, to serve

Serves 4

Wipe the mushrooms. Select some of the smallest ones and take a slice from the centre of each. Set aside the slices. Chop the rest coarsely.

In a frying pan, heat the butter to sizzling, then fry the chopped mushrooms, seasoning well to taste. Leave to cool, then purée in a blender or food processor with the garlic and 250 ml (8 fl oz) of the stock.

Pour the remaining stock into a large pan. Add the mushroom purée and heat to simmering. Stir in the cream. Add the reserved mushroom slices and simmer for 5 minutes. Taste and adjust seasoning, if necessary.

Serve hot with crusty French bread.

Italian Ribollita

2 tablespoons olive oil
2 onions, finely chopped
2 carrots, finely chopped
2 sticks celery, finely chopped
2 garlic cloves, crushed
3 tablespoons fresh parsley, chopped
2 zucchini (courgettes), finely chopped
225 g (8 oz) spinach, washed and stems removed
6 large tomatoes, diced
750 ml (1¼ pints/3 cups) water
2 tablespoons tomato paste
salt and freshly ground black pepper, to taste
3 slices day-old white bread, torn into pieces
Parmesan, grated, to garnish

Serves 6

Heat the oil in a large pan over medium heat. Add the onions, carrots, celery, garlic and parsley. Sauté over a medium heat for 7 minutes, or until the vegetables are soft. Add the zucchini, spinach and tomatoes with the water and tomato paste.

Cover and cook for 20 minutes, or until the vegetables are mushy. Season with salt and pepper. Add the bread and cook for another 20 minutes.

Serve garnished with Parmesan.

Lentil Soup

175 g (6 oz/1 cup) brown
    lentils, rinsed
2 tablespoons olive oil
1 large onion, finely sliced
2 garlic cloves, finely chopped
3 rashers (strips) bacon, rind
    discarded, and meat diced
400 g (14 oz) can tomatoes
    with basil
400 g (14 oz) can tomatoes
1 teaspoon dried basil
1.5 litres (2½ pints) beef stock
crusty bread, to serve

Serves 6

Cover the lentils in water to soak while preparing the other ingredients.

Heat the oil in a large pan and cook the onion and garlic until transparent. Add the bacon and cook lightly.

Drain the lentils and add to the pan with the tomatoes including the juice, basil and stock. Cover and cook for 1–1½ hours, or until the lentils are tender. Serve hot with crusty bread.

Minestrone

55 g (2 oz) butter
2 garlic cloves, crushed
2 small onions, finely chopped
4 rashers (strips) bacon, rind
   removed and meat chopped
115 g (4 oz) can red kidney beans
100 g (3½ oz) green beans,
   trimmed
½ small cabbage, roughly
   chopped
3 medium potatoes, peeled and
   chopped
2 medium carrots, peeled and
   diced
150 g (5 oz) fresh or frozen peas,
   shelled
1 stick celery, chopped
2 tablespoons fresh parsley, finely
   chopped
2 litres (3½ pints) chicken stock
salt, to taste
100 g (3½ oz) spinach, washed
   and chopped
50 g (1¾ oz) pasta
Parmesan, shaved, to serve

Serves 4

In a deep pan, heat the butter and add the garlic, onion and bacon. Sauté for 4–5 minutes until the onion is soft.

Add all the other ingredients to the pan, except for the spinach and pasta, and bring to the boil. Reduce the heat and allow the mixture to simmer, covered, for about 90 minutes.

Stir in the spinach, then the pasta, and cook until the pasta is *al dente*, about 15 minutes. Serve with shaved Parmesan.

Mussel, White Wine and Roasted Tomato Soup

1.5 kg (3¼ lb) mussels

310 g (11 oz) tomatoes, halved

75 ml (2½ fl oz/⅓ cup) olive oil

1 brown onion, chopped

4 garlic cloves, crushed

75 ml (2½ fl oz/⅓ cup) white wine

400 g (14 oz) can tomatoes, peeled

55 g (2 oz) tomato paste

75 ml (2½ fl oz/⅓ cup) fish stock, or water

2 tablespoons fresh oregano, chopped

salt and freshly ground black pepper, to taste

crusty Italian bread, to serve

Serves 4–6

Preheat the oven to 220°C (425°F/Gas mark 7).

Wash the mussels under cold running water, scrub the shells with a scourer, and remove their beards. Discard any mussels that are open.

Place the tomatoes on a baking tray, drizzle with a little olive oil, sprinkle with salt, and roast in the oven for 20 minutes.

Heat the remaining oil in a pan and sauté the onion and garlic until soft. Add the white wine and cook for 2 minutes. Add the roasted tomatoes, can of tomatoes, tomato paste, stock (or water) and oregano, and simmer for 5–10 minutes. Season with salt and pepper.

Add the mussels, cover, and cook for another 5 minutes, until the mussels have opened. Discard any that do not open.

Serve with crusty Italian bread.

Potato and Leek Soup with Pancetta

30 g (1 oz) butter

150 g (5 oz) pancetta, cut into strips

1 brown onion, chopped

450 g (1 lb) potatoes, peeled and cut into chunks

750 ml (1¼ pints/3 cups) chicken stock

1 large leek, washed and sliced

1 bay leaf

75 ml (2½ fl oz/¹/₃ cup) single (light(cream, optional

1 teaspoon nutmeg

salt and freshly ground black pepper, to taste

45 g (1½ oz/½ cup) Parmesan, grated

Serves 4–6

Melt the butter in a large pan, add the pancetta, and sauté for 5 minutes until the pancetta is crisp.

Add the onion and cook for another 5 minutes until the onion is starting to soften. Add the potatoes and cook for 10 minutes making sure the potatoes do not stick to the base of the pan.

Add the chicken stock, leek and bay leaf, and bring to the boil. Reduce the heat, simmer for 45 minutes, or until the potatoes are cooked. Remove the bay leaf, add the cream and nutmeg, and season with salt and pepper.

Stir through the Parmesan, and serve.

Pumpkin and Split Pea Soup

2 tablespoons olive oil

1 onion, chopped

2 garlic cloves, crushed

175 g (6 oz/1 cup) yellow split
    peas

1.25 litres (2¼ pints) cold
    chicken stock

450 g (1 lb) pumpkin, peeled,
    de-seeded and cut into
    small chunks

salt and freshly ground
    pepper, to taste

pinch of ground nutmeg

basil pesto, to garnish

Serves 4

Heat the oil in a large pan. Add the onion and garlic and sauté until clear. Add the split peas and chicken stock. Bring to the boil then add the pumpkin.

Cover and simmer for 30–40 minutes, or until the peas are tender and the pumpkin is breaking up. Mix to break up the pumpkin. Season to taste with salt, pepper and nutmeg. Serve hot, garnished with a swirl of pesto.

Roasted Aubergine Soup

900 g (2 lb) eggplant
  (aubergines), halved
4 red bell peppers
  (capsicums), halved
1 teaspoon olive oil
2 garlic cloves, crushed
4 tomatoes, peeled and
  chopped
750 ml (1¼ pints/3 cups)
  vegetable stock
2 teaspoons black
  peppercorns, crushed

Serves 6

Place the aubergine and capsicum skin side up under a hot grill (broiler) and cook for 10 minutes, or until the flesh is soft and the skins are blackened. When cool enough to handle, peel away and discard the blackened skin and roughly chop the flesh.

Heat the oil in a large pan over a medium heat. Add the garlic and tomatoes and cook, stirring, for 2 minutes. Add the aubergine, bell peppers, stock and black peppercorns, bring to a simmer and leave for 4 minutes. Remove the pan from the heat and set aside to cool slightly.

Place the vegetables and stock in batches in a food processor or blender and process until smooth. Return the mixture to a clean pan, bring to a simmer over a medium heat, and cook for 3–5 minutes, or until heated through. Serve hot.

Note: This soup can be made the day before and reheated when required.

Roasted Tomato, Red Capsicum and Bread Soup

900 g (2 lb) Roma tomatoes,
  halved
2 red bell peppers
  (capsicums), halved
3 tablespoons olive oil
2 onions, finely chopped
3 garlic cloves, crushed
2 teaspoons ground cumin
1 teaspoon ground coriander
1 litre (1¾ pints/4 cups)
  chicken stock
2 slices white bread, crusts
  discarded and bread torn
  into pieces
1 tablespoon balsamic vinegar
salt and freshly ground black
  pepper, to taste
Parmesan, grated, to serve

Serves 4

Preheat the oven to 220°C (425°F/Gas mark 7).

Place the tomatoes and capsicums (skin side up) on a lightly oiled baking tray and bake for 20 minutes, or until the skins have blistered. Set aside to cool, then remove the skins and roughly chop.

Heat the remaining oil in a pan, add the onion and garlic, and cook for 5 minutes, or until soft. Add the cumin and coriander, and cook for 1 minute, until well combined. Add the tomatoes, capsicums and stock to the pan, bring to the boil, and simmer for 30 minutes. Add the bread, balsamic vinegar and salt and pepper, and cook for another 5–10 minutes.

Serve with Parmesan.

Sweet Potato and Rosemary Soup

3 tablespoons olive oil

2 garlic cloves, crushed

1 medium onion, chopped

1 tablespoon fresh rosemary,
  chopped, plus extra to serve

2 tablespoons tomato pesto

1 medium carrot, peeled and
  diced

1 large potato, peeled and
  diced

750 g (1 lb 10 oz) sweet
  potato, diced

1 litre (1¾ pints/4 cups)
  chicken stock

salt and freshly ground black
  pepper, to taste

Serves 4–6

Heat the oil in a pan, add the garlic, onion and rosemary, and cook over medium heat for 3–5 minutes, or until soft. Add the pesto, and cook for 1 minute. Add the carrot, potato and sweet potato and cook another 5 minutes.

Add the chicken stock, salt and pepper, and bring to the boil, then reduce the heat, and simmer with the lid on for 30–40 minutes, or until the vegetables are soft.

Purée the soup in a food processor or blender. You may have to do this in two batches. Return the soup to the pan, add the remaining rosemary, and heat through before serving.

Add extra stock if the soup is too thick.

Tomato Soup

1 lb 10 oz (750 g) ripe
   tomatoes, chopped
1 potato, peeled and chopped
1 small onion, chopped
1 sprig fresh basil
1 teaspoon sugar
2 tablespoons tomato paste
salt and freshly ground black
   pepper
250 ml (8 fl oz/1 cup)
   vegetable stock
60 ml (2 fl oz/¼ cup) double
   (heavy) cream
1 tablespoon parsley, finely
   chopped

Serves 4

Place all the ingredients except for the parsley and cream into a large pan with the stock. Bring to the boil and simmer, covered, for 20 minutes.

Serve the soup with a swirl of cream and sprinkle with chopped parsley.

Tuscan Bean Soup

2 garlic cloves
¼ teaspoon salt
2 tablespoons olive oil
1 onion, finely chopped
3 sticks celery, sliced
1 leek, sliced
2 carrots, peeled and
   chopped
175 g (6 oz) tomato paste
400 g (14 oz) can tomatoes
250 ml (8 fl oz/1 cup) beef
   stock
250 ml (8 fl oz/1 cup) water
1 teaspoon dried thyme
175 g (6 oz/1 cup) green
   (French) beans, trimmed
225 g (8 oz) spinach, washed,
   stems removed and
   shredded
salt and freshly ground black
   pepper, to taste
crusty Italian bread, to serve

Serves 6

Crush the garlic and mash with the salt.

Heat the oil in a large pan. Add the garlic mixture, onion, celery, leek and carrot. Cover and cook, shaking the pan frequently, until the vegetables are golden. Stir in the tomato paste, tomatoes with their juice, stock, water and thyme. Bring to the boil, cover and cook gently for 45 minutes.

Meanwhile, cook the beans in boiling water until just tender. Drain the beans reserving half a cup of the cooking liquid. Put all but a quarter of the beans into a blender or food processor with the reserved liquid and process until very finely chopped. Add the processed beans and the spinach to the soup and continue cooking for 15 minutes, then add the whole cooked beans. Cook for another 5 minutes.

Season with salt and pepper and serve with crusty bread.

White Bean and Chorizo Soup

1 tablespoon butter

2 onions, roughly chopped

3 garlic cloves, crushed

2 carrots, peeled and
   chopped

2 sticks celery, sliced

1 bouquet garni

1 litre (1¾ pints/4 cups)
   chicken stock

400 g (14 oz) can cannellini
   beans, drained

1 chorizo, cooked and cut into
   1 cm (½ in) slices, to garnish

salt and freshly ground black
   pepper, to taste

Serves 4

Heat the butter in a large pan, then add the onion, garlic, carrots and celery and sauté for 10 minutes, taking care that the vegetables do not colour. Add the bouquet garni and chicken stock. Bring to the boil and simmer for 10 minutes. Add the beans and stir through. Remove the bouquet garni and allow the soup to cool slightly. Pureé the mixture in a blender or food processor until smooth.

Return the soup to the pan and reheat gently. Serve hot garnished with chorizo and seasoned with salt and pepper.

VEGETABLES

Mixed Beans with Pine Nuts and Parmesan

250 g (9 oz) yellow (dwarf French) beans, trimmed

200 g (7 oz) green beans, trimmed

2 tablespoons red wine vinegar

1 teaspoon honey

1 garlic clove, crushed

2 tablespoon fresh mint, finely chopped

1 tablespoon mustard seed oil

2 tablespoons pine nuts, toasted

2 tablespoons Parmesan, shaved

freshly ground black pepper, to taste

Serves 4

Steam the beans until tender. Do not overcook or they will lose their colour. Drain well.

In a bowl, whisk together the red wine vinegar, honey, garlic, mint and mustard seed oil in a small bowl.

Pour the dressing over the beans, top with toasted pine nuts and pepper.

Brussels Sprouts with Almond Pesto

450 g (1 lb) Brussels sprouts,
   washed and trimmed
30 g (1 oz/¼ cup) flaked
   almonds, toasted

Almond Pesto
15 g (½ oz/¼ cup) tightly
   packed fresh basil
½ garlic clove, crushed
pinch of salt
2 tablespoons olive oil
30 g (1 oz/¼ cup) toasted
   almonds
15 g (½ oz) Parmesan, grated
   (shredded)

Serves 4

To make the almond pesto, place the basil in a mortar, add the garlic, salt and half the oil. Pound the mixture with the pestle to make a smooth paste. Add the almonds and remaining oil and pound again until the nuts are lightly chopped. Mix in the Parmesan.

Steam the Brussels sprouts until just tender. Drain well. Toss through the almond pesto and garnish with toasted flaked almonds.

Roasted Garlic with Thyme

3 whole bulbs of garlic
60 ml (2 fl oz/¼ cup) olive oil
1 tablespoon thyme, chopped

Preheat the oven to 180°C (350°F/Gas mark 4).

To roast the garlic, slice off the tops of the bulbs to expose the tips of the cloves. Place cut-side up in a roasting pan. Drizzle with a little olive oil, and sprinkle with thyme.

Cover with foil and roast for 45–60 minutes, or until soft, golden brown and quite fragrant.

Allow to cool, then squeeze the garlic out of the cloves, leave to cool, wrap in plastic wrap (cling film) and refrigerate (for up to 1 week).

Italian Roast Vegetables

2 garlic cloves, finely chopped

60 ml (2 fl oz/¼ cup) olive oil

8 asparagus spears, with thick
ends snapped off

3 zucchini (courgettes), cut
into quarters lengthways

1 red bell pepper (capsicum),
pith and seeds removed
and thinly sliced

6 mushrooms, halved

15 g (½ oz) fresh basil,
chopped

Serves 4–6

Preheat the oven to 200°C (400°F/Gas mark 6).

Mix the garlic with the oil and pour into a roasting dish. Place the vegetables in the roasting dish and toss in oil. Roast for 15 minutes, or until the vegetables are tender and start to brown. Remove from the oven and cool slightly. Toss through the basil and serve warm.

Baked Potatoes with Rosemary

900 g (2 lb) potatoes, peeled
and quartered
1 tablespoon olive oil
½ teaspoon sea salt
1 tablespoon fresh rosemary,
chopped

Serves 4

Preheat the oven to 200°C (400°F/Gas mark 6).

Place the potatoes in a baking dish, and mix in the oil, salt and rosemary. Bake in the oven for 45–60 minutes. Serve hot.

Italian Baked Potatoes

6 medium potatoes, peeled
400 g (14 oz) can tomatoes
225 g (8 oz) mozzarella
cheese, grated
55 g (2 oz) Parmesan, grated
2 tablespoons fresh basil,
chopped
3 tablespoons olive oil
30 g (1 oz) soft breadcrumbs

Serves 4–6

Preheat the oven to 190°C (375°F/Gas mark 5).

Cook the potatoes in boiling salted water for 10 minutes. Drain well. Cool, then cut into thick slices. Arrange a layer of potatoes over the base of a greased shallow baking dish. Pour over half the tomatoes and sprinkle over half the cheeses and 1 tablespoon of basil. Pour over 1 tablespoon of the oil. Repeat the layers.

Sprinkle with breadcrumbs and the remaining oil and bake for 30 minutes, or until the potatoes are tender and the breadcrumbs are golden brown.

Parmesan Potatoes

400 g (14 oz) potatoes, peeled
  and diced
1 tablespoon olive oil
1 tablespoon butter
1 tablespoon Parmesan,
  grated (shredded)
salt

Serves 4

Put the potatoes in a pan and cover with salted water. Bring to the boil over high heat and cook until just a little hard in the centre. Drain.

Heat the oil and butter in a pan, add the potatoes, and cook until brown. Add the cheese, and cook, until the potatoes are crisp.

Tuscan Potatoes

60 ml (2 fl oz/¼ cup) olive oil
6 medium potatoes, peeled
  and cut into chunks
4 garlic cloves, finely chopped
1½ teaspoons dried rosemary
freshly ground black pepper,
  to taste

Serves 4

Preheat the oven to 190°C (375°F/Gas mark 5).

Heat the oil in a roasting pan. Add the potatoes, garlic and rosemary. Bake for 30–40 minutes, or until the potatoes are cooked, turning them frequently during cooking.

Arrange on a serving plate and grind over black pepper before serving.

Sage Butter Zucchini

6 zucchini (courgettes),
    trimmed and cut into 2 cm
    (¾ in) pieces
30 g (1 oz) butter
2 tablespoons fresh sage,
    chopped
2 tablespoons Parmesan,
    grated (shredded)
2 tablespoons pine nuts,
    roasted
salt and freshly ground black
    pepper, to taste

Serves 4

Steam the zucchini until just cooked. Place in a serving dish.

Heat the butter in a small pan, add the sage and cook until the butter browns. Sprinkle over the Parmesan and pine nuts. Season with salt and pepper.

Pour the butter mixture over the zucchini and serve immediately.

Zucchini and Mint Moulds with Fresh Tomato Sauce

6 zucchini (courgettes),
  trimmed and coarsely
  grated (shredded)
1 tablespoon salt
1 tablespoon fresh mint,
  chopped
1 tablespoon fresh chives,
  chopped
freshly ground black pepper,
  to taste
1 tomato, de-seeded and
  flesh diced

Fresh Tomato Sauce
1 tablespoon olive oil
1 onion, finely chopped
2 garlic cloves, crushed
6 tomatoes, cores removed
  and roughly chopped
15 g/½ oz fresh basil,
  chopped

Serves 4

Place the zucchini in a sieve and sprinkle with the salt. Leave to drain for 30 minutes to 1 hour.

Squeeze the zucchini and mix with the mint, chives, pepper and tomato. Pack the zucchini mixture into six small ramekins and refrigerate until ready to serve. .

To make the fresh tomato sauce, heat the oil in a pan and sauté the onion and garlic for 5 minutes, or until translucent. Add the tomatoes and basil and cook for another 5 minutes, breaking up the tomato with a wooden spoon. Leave chunky or purée in a sieve or blender to serve. Serve warm or cold with the zucchini.

RICE and POLENTA

Risotto Milanese

1 litre (1¾ pints/4 cups)
  chicken stock
2 tablespoons olive oil
1 onion, finely chopped
1 garlic clove, crushed
400 g (14 oz/2 cups) arborio
  rice
250 ml (8 fl oz/1 cup) white
  wine
55 g (2 oz) pecorino cheese,
  grated (shredded)
2 tablespoons parsley, finely
  chopped

Serves 6

Heat the chicken stock in a pan, reduce the heat, and leave simmering.

Heat the oil in a heavy pan, add the onion and garlic, and cook, until soft.

Add the rice, and stir, until coated with the mixture. Add the wine and cook until the wine has been absorbed, stirring continuously.

Add the chicken stock, a ladle at a time, stirring continuously. Wait until the liquid has been absorbed, before adding another ladle of stock. Continue adding stock a ladle at a time until all the stock is used, and until the rice is cooked, but still firm to the bite. It may be necessary to add a little more liquid.

Stir in the cheese and parsley and serve immediately.

Risotto with Baby Spinach and Gorgonzola

1 litre (1¾ pints/4 cups)
  chicken stock
2 tablespoons olive oil
2 garlic cloves, crushed
1 onion, finely chopped
400 g (14 oz/2 cups) arborio
  rice
125 ml (4 fl oz/½ cup) white
  wine
225 g (8 oz) baby spinach
225 g (8 oz) Gorgonzola, in
  small pieces
salt and freshly ground black
  pepper, to taste

Serves 6

Place the stock in a pan and bring to the boil. Leave simmering.

Heat the oil in a large pan, add the garlic and onion, and cook for 5 minutes, or until soft. Add the rice, and stir, until well coated.

Pour in the wine and cook, until the liquid has been absorbed. Add the stock, a ladle at a time, stirring continuously, until the liquid has been absorbed, before adding the next ladle of stock. Keep adding stock in this way, and stirring, until all stock is used, and until the rice is cooked, but still firm to the bite.

Add the spinach, cheese and seasonings. Stir and cook until the spinach is just wilted and the cheese has melted. Serve immediately.

Garlic and Capocollo Risotto

1 bulb garlic, roasted

225 g (8 oz) broad (fava)
  beans

14 thin slices capocollo

1 tablespoon olive oil

1 small onion, finely diced

400 g (14 oz/2 cups) arborio
  rice

2 tablespoons white wine

1.5 litres (2½ pints) chicken
  stock

25 g (¾ oz) butter

45 g/1½ oz Parmesan, grated
  (shredded)

Serves 4

Preheat the oven to 200ºC/400°F/Gas mark 6. Wrap the garlic bulb tightly in foil and roast in the oven for 50 minutes.

Scald the broad beans in boiling water, then quickly plunge in ice-cold water and drain. Remove the beans from their skins.

Dice 8 slices of the capocollo.

Squeeze the garlic out of the skin and set aside.

Heat a heavy pan. Add the olive oil and fry the onion and capocollo for 3 minutes, stirring constantly. Add the rice and continue to stir for another 3 minutes. Add the roasted garlic and the white wine, then add the stock one cup at a time, stirring constantly. Continue until all the stock is absorbed: approximately 20 minutes.

Stir through the butter, Parmesan and broad beans and cook for 2 more minutes. Season to taste and garnish with the remaining capocollo slices.

Italian Mushroom Risotto

85 g (3 oz) butter

1 onion, finely chopped

1 garlic clove, crushed

250 g (9 oz) mushrooms,
  sliced

400 g (14 oz/2 cups) arborio
  rice

125 ml (4 fl oz/½ cup) dry
  white wine

1 tablespoon tomato paste

300 ml (½ pint) vegetable
  stock, heated

Parmesan shavings, to serve

Serves 4

In a frying pan set over medium heat, add the butter, onion and garlic and cook until the onion is golden. Add the mushrooms and cook over low heat for 2 minutes.

Add the rice to the pan and cook over a medium heat, stirring constantly for 3 minutes, or until the rice becomes translucent. Add the wine and tomato paste, stirring until absorbed. Pour half a cup of hot stock into the rice mixture and cook, stirring constantly, until the liquid is absorbed. Continue cooking in this way until all the stock is used.

Remove from the heat, add the Parmesan and toss with fork to blend.

Roasted Pumpkin Risotto

1 lb 2 oz (500 g) butternut
   pumpkin, peeled and cut
   into 2 cm (¾ in) pieces
2 tablespoons olive oil
2 teaspoons balsamic vinegar
salt and freshly ground black
   pepper
1¼ litres (generous 2 pints)
   vegetable stock
1 onion, finely chopped
3 garlic cloves, crushed
400 g (14 oz/2 cups) arborio
   rice
1 teaspoon dried rosemary
   leaves
115 g (4 oz) goat's cheese,
   crumbled
150 g (5 oz) baby spinach
   leaves, washed and
   trimmed
15 g (½ oz) fresh parsley,
   chopped
crusty bread, to serve

Serves 4

Preheat the oven to 220°C (425°F/Gas mark 7).

Combine the pumpkin, 1 tablespoon of the olive oil, the balsamic vinegar, salt and pepper in a non-stick baking tray. Bake for 20–25 minutes, or until the pumpkin is golden.

Meanwhile, place the vegetable stock in a pan. Bring to a boil and simmer gently. Heat the remaining oil in a large pan over medium heat. Cook the onion and garlic for 2–3 minutes or until soft. Add the rice and stir until combined.

Add 1 cup of the stock and the rosemary leaves to the rice. Cook, stirring from time to time, until all the liquid is absorbed. Repeat this until all the stock is used and the rice is tender.

Stir in the pumpkin, goat's cheese, baby spinach and parsley and season to taste. Cook until heated through and the spinach has wilted. Serve immediately with crusty bread.

Risotto Tricolore

2 tablespoons olive oil

4 garlic cloves, finely chopped

2 red bell peppers
(capsicums), cut into $1/8$ in
(3 mm) slices

2 yellow bell peppers
(capsicums), cut into $1/8$ in
(3 mm) slices

2 green bell peppers
(capsicums), cut into $1/8$ in
(3 mm) slices

400 g (14 oz/2 cups) arborio
rice

125 ml (4 fl oz/$1/2$ cup) dry
white wine

875 ml (28 fl oz/$3^1/2$ cups)
vegetable stock, heated

45 g ($1^1/2$ oz) butter

15 g ($1/2$ oz) parsley, chopped

freshly ground black pepper

Serves 4

Heat the olive oil in a pan and cook the garlic gently. Add the bell peppers and continue cooking for 5 minutes. Add the rice and stir to coat. Add the wine and allow all the liquid to be absorbed.

Pour 1 cup of hot stock into the rice mixture and cook, stirring constantly, until the liquid is absorbed. Continue cooking in this way until all the stock is used and the rice is tender.

Remove the risotto from the heat and add the butter, parsley and black pepper. Stir well and serve immediately.

Artichoke Risotto

55 g (2 oz) butter

1 onion, chopped

280 g (10½ oz/1½ cups) arborio rice

500 ml (16 fl oz/2 cups) chicken stock

125 ml (4 fl oz/½ cup) dry white wine

400 g (14 oz) can artichoke hearts, drained and liquid reserved

2 tablespoons fresh parsley, chopped

4 thick slices ham, cut into strips

55 g (2 oz) Parmesan, shaved

4 cherry tomatoes, quartered

freshly ground black pepper, to taste

Serves 4

Melt the butter in a large frying pan, and add the onion and cook for 5 minutes, or until soft.

Add the rice to the pan and cook, stirring frequently, for 5 minutes. Combine stock, wine and reserved artichoke liquid. The total amount of liquid should equal 875 ml (28 fl oz/ 3½ cups). Top up with more stock if necessary.

Pour one-third of the liquid over the rice and cook over a low heat, stirring, until the liquid is absorbed. Continue adding liquid a little at a time and cook, stirring frequently, until all the liquid is absorbed and the rice is cooked.

Cut the artichokes into quarters. Fold the artichokes, parsley, ham, Parmesan and tomatoes into the rice. Season with pepper and serve immediately.

Saffron and Chicken Risotto

1 litre (1¾ pints/4 cups)
  vegetable stock
250 ml (8 fl oz/1 cup) dry
  white wine
1 tablespoon vegetable oil
2 boneless chicken breast
  fillets, sliced
45 g (1½ oz) butter
3 leeks, sliced
400 g (14 oz/2 cups) arborio
  rice
pinch of saffron threads
55 g (2 oz) Parmesan, grated
freshly ground black pepper,
  to taste

Serves 4

Place the stock and wine in a pan and bring to the boil over a medium heat. Reduce the heat and keep warm.

Heat the oil in a pan over a medium heat, add the chicken and cook, stirring, for 5 minutes, or until the chicken is tender. Remove the chicken from the pan and set aside.

Add the butter and leeks to the same pan and cook over a low heat, stirring, for 8 minutes, or until the leeks are golden and caramelised.

Add the rice and saffron to the pan and cook over a medium heat, stirring constantly, for 3 minutes, or until the rice becomes translucent. Pour 250 ml (8 fl oz/1 cup) hot stock mixture into the rice mixture and cook, stirring constantly, until the liquid is absorbed. Continue cooking in this way until all the stock is used and the rice is tender.

Stir the chicken, Parmesan and black pepper, to taste, into the risotto and cook for 2 minutes more. Serve immediately.

Scallop and Tomato Risotto

400 g (14 oz) arborio rice

1 litre (1¾ pints/4 cups) fish
  stock, heated

20 scallops, roe removed

8 Roma tomatoes, diced

Serves 4

Preheat a medium pan over medium-low heat. Add the rice and cook, stirring, for 1 minute. Reduce the heat to low, add a ladleful of hot stock and cook, stirring constantly, until the liquid is absorbed. Continue cooking in this way until all the stock is used and the rice is creamy and tender.

Heat a large non-stick frying pan on medium-high heat. Cook the scallops for 1 minute on each side, then transfer to a medium bowl.

Add the tomatoes and scallops to the risotto and stir through to warm and combine.

Mussel Risotto

2 tablespoons olive oil

1 onion, finely chopped

2 garlic cloves, finely chopped

1 red bell pepper (capsicum),
   diced

280 g (10½ oz/1½ cups)
   arborio rice

625 ml (generous 1 pint/
   2½ cups) dry white wine

1 kg (2¼ lb) mussels, cleaned

1 sprig rosemary, leaves
   removed and chopped

2 sprigs thyme, leaves
   removed and stalks
   discarded

45 g (1½ oz) Parmesan,
   shaved

Serves 4

Place the oil in a pan over medium heat. Add the onion, garlic and bell pepper and cook for 2 minutes.

Add the rice and half the wine, stirring constantly until the liquid is absorbed. Add the mussels and the rest of the wine.

Add the herbs, cover and cook until the rice and mussels are cooked, stirring frequently. Discard any mussels that do not open. Serve garnished Parmesan.

Seafood Risotto

125 ml (4 fl oz/½ cup) olive oil
1 medium onion, chopped
2 garlic cloves, chopped
3 cups (1 lb 5 oz) arborio rice
1 bunch shallots, chopped
30 g (1 oz) fresh coriander
  (cilantro), chopped
1 small butternut pumpkin,
  cut into small chunks and
  cooked
1.5 litres (2.5 pints) fish stock
250 ml (8 fl oz/1 cup) white
  wine
900 g (2 lb) marinara mix
  (mussels, fish, oysters,
  shrimp (prawns), squid)
70 g (2¼ oz/¾ cup)
  Parmesan, shaved, plus
  extra to garnish
salt and freshly ground black
  pepper, to taste
3 tablespoons sour cream

Serves 6

Heat the oil in a large pan and gently fry the onion and garlic. When the onion is translucent, add the rice. Stir well, until the rice is coated with oil. Add the shallots and coriander and cook for a few minutes, then add the pumpkin.

Add a ladleful of stock, stirring constantly until the liquid is absorbed into the rice. Add the wine and stir. Continue to add stock a ladleful at a time and stir regularly, until all the stock is absorbed, about 30 minutes.

When the rice is almost cooked, fold in the marinara mix and cook for another 5 minutes. Add the Parmesan. Season with salt and pepper. Cook for another few minutes, until the seafood is cooked through, then stir in the sour cream.

Serve in bowls, with extra Parmesan, if you like.

Shrimp Risotto

4 tablespoons olive oil

2 small onions, finely chopped

225 g (8 oz) arborio rice

175 ml (6 fl oz/¾ cup) dry
  white wine

1 litre (1¾ pints/4 cups) fish
  stock

1 medium onion, grated
  (shredded)

450 g (1 lb) green shrimp
  (prawns), shelled

squeeze of lemon juice

fresh parsley, chopped, to
  garnish

zest of 1 lemon, to garnish

Serves 4

Place half of the oil in a frying pan and lightly brown the onions. Add the rice and cook, stirring constantly, until lightly browned. Add the wine. When the wine has evaporated, add the stock gradually, a ladleful at a time. Allow the rice to absorb the liquid before adding more stock. Stir very lightly and simmer gently, uncovered, until the rice is cooked. Add a little hot water or more wine if the rice gets too dry.

Meanwhile, heat the remaining oil in a pan and add the grated onion, lemon juice and chopped shrimp. Fry lightly until the onion is translucent and the shrimp are cooked, approximately 5 minutes. Stir through the rice and serve sprinkled with parsley and lemon zest.

Bacon and Pea Risotto

3 rashers (strips) rindless
  bacon, cut into thin strips
1 onion, finely chopped
300 g (10½ oz/1½ cup)
  arborio rice
1 teaspoon dried sage
1.2 litres (2 pints/5 cups)
  chicken stock, heated
225 g (8 oz/2 cups) frozen
  peas
freshly ground black pepper
45 g (1½ oz) Parmesan

Serves 4

In a large pan set over medium heat, sauté the bacon and onion for about 5 minutes, or until the onion is soft.

Add the rice and sage and stir to coat the rice in the bacon and onion mixture.

Pour a ladleful of hot stock into the rice mixture and cook, stirring constantly, until the liquid is absorbed. Repeat with another ladleful of stock.

Continue adding stock 1 ladleful at a time until the rice is tender and all the liquid has been absorbed. With the last addition of stock, add the peas.

When all the stock is absorbed, season the risotto with pepper and ladle into bowls. Top with Parmesan shavings and serve immediately.

Tuna, Vegetable and Rice Fritters

185 g (6 oz) can tuna in olive
  oil
1 large onion, finely chopped
2 eggs
1 carrot, grated
250 g (9 oz) cooked
  wholegrain rice
55 g (2 oz/½ cup) plain (all-
  purpose) flour
salt and pepper, to taste

Serves 4

Combine all the ingredients.
  Mix well and add enough water to create a batter.
  Fry dessertspoons of the mixture in hot oil for approximately
3 minutes, or until golden.
  Serve with lemon wedges.

Aubergine with Rice and Cheese Filling

2 eggplants (aubergines), cut in half lengthways
salt

Rice and Cheese Filling
2 tablespoons olive oil
1 onion, chopped
1 garlic clove, crushed
2 rashers (strips) bacon, rind removed and chopped
3 x 400 g (14 oz) cans diced tomatoes, drained
1 teaspoon fresh thyme, chopped
1 egg
55 g (2 oz/1 cup) dried breadcrumbs
75 g (2½ oz/¹/₃ cup) rice, cooked
55 g (2 oz) Parmesan, shaved

Serves 4

Scoop out the centre of the eggplants leaving a 2 cm (¾ in) thick shell. Sprinkle with salt, place upside down on paper towels and set aside for 15 minutes.

Preheat the oven to 180°C (350°F/Gas mark 4).

Rinse the eggplant and pat dry with paper towels.

To make the filling, place the oil, onion, garlic, bacon, tomatoes, thyme, egg, breadcrumbs, rice and cheese in a bowl and mix to combine. Divide the mixture between the eggplant shells, place in a lightly greased baking dish, and bake for 30 minutes. Serve hot.

Baked Polenta with Basil and Garlic

750 ml (1¼ pints/3 cups)
   chicken stock
150 g (5 oz/1 cup) instant
   polenta
1 garlic clove, crushed
2 tablespoons fresh basil,
   chopped
45 g (1½ oz) pecorino cheese,
   grated
salt and freshly ground black
   pepper, to taste

Makes 8 triangles

Grease a 25 x 20 cm (10 x 8 in) heatproof baking dish. Preheat the oven to 180°C (350°F/Gas mark 4).

Pour the stock into a pan, bring to the boil, gradually pour in the polenta, stirring continuously for 5–10 minutes, or until it comes away from pan.

Take the polenta off the heat and add the garlic, basil, cheese, salt and pepper. Pour the polenta into the greased dish, and press evenly over the base. Bake for 30 minutes.

Serve cut into triangles.

Polenta with Mozzarella, Prosciutto and Tomato

150 g (5 oz/1 cup) instant
   polenta
250 ml (8 fl oz/1 cup) cold
   water
375 ml (12 fl oz/1½ cups)
   boiling water
1½ teaspoons salt
1 garlic clove
1 tablespoon olive oil, plus
   extra for greasing

Topping
8 slices mozzarella cheese
8 slices prosciutto
8 slices tomato
1 teaspoon dried basil

Serves 4

Mix the polenta and cold water in a pan. Stir in the boiling water and salt and cook over medium heat for 10 minutes. Continue to cook over a low heat for 15 minutes, stirring occasionally to prevent sticking.

Spread the polenta into a greased 18 cm (7 in) shallow square baking dish. Cut polenta into squares. Brush with oil, rub with garlic and grill (broil) on one side. Top each polenta square with a slice of cheese, prosciutto and tomato. Sprinkle with basil and top with the remaining cheese. Grill for 1 minute and serve.

Polenta and Corn Fritters

375 ml (12 fl oz/1½ cups)
 water
½ teaspoon salt
75 g (2½ oz/½ cup) instant
 polenta
115 g (4 oz) sweetcorn kernels
75 g (¾ oz/¼ cup) spring
 onions (scallions), finely
 sliced
1 tablespoon parsley, finely
 chopped
1 small garlic clove, crushed
45 g (1½ oz/⅓ cup) plain (all-
 purpose) flour
¼ teaspoon baking powder
1 egg, lightly beaten
salt and freshly ground black
 pepper, to taste
olive oil, for frying pan

Makes 16 fritters

In a pan, bring the water and salt to the boil, and gradually add the polenta, stirring continuously for 3–5 minutes, or until the polenta is thick and comes together like glue.

Take off the heat and add the sweetcorn, spring onions, parsley and garlic. Stir until combined. Transfer to a bowl, and leave to cool.

Sift the flour and baking powder together, and combine with the polenta mixture. Add the egg and salt and pepper.

Heat the oil in a frying pan, and set over medium to high heat. Place tablespoons of the mixture in the pan. Flatten into fritters and cook for 1–2 minutes on each side.

Roasted Garlic Polenta

2 bulbs garlic

1 shallot, finely diced

1 teaspoon salt

1.5 litres (2¼ pints) water

225 g (8 oz) fast cooking
polenta

50 g (1¾ oz) butter

50 g (1¾ oz) Parmesan,
shaved

15 g (½ oz) bunch basil,
chopped

chargrilled vegetables, to
serve

Serves 4

Preheat the oven to 200°C/400°F/Gas mark 6. Wrap the garlic in foil and roast it for 45 minutes to 1 hour. Remove from the oven and squeeze out the garlic from the skins.

Place the shallot, salt and water into a large pan and bring to the boil. Pour the polenta into the boiling water and stir continuously for 5 minutes.

Stir the garlic through the polenta. Stir through the butter and Parmesan. Cook for 2 minutes. Serve topped with basil accompanied by chargrilled vegetables.

Courgette Polenta Slices

15 g (½ oz) butter
3 tablespoons olive oil
250 g (9 oz) zucchini
  (courgette), grated
  (shredded)
750 ml (1¼ pints/3 cups)
  vegetable stock
175 g (6 oz) instant polenta
salt and black pepper
40 g (1½ oz) Parmesan,
  shaved

Serves 4

Lightly butter a shallow 22 cm (8½ in) square roasting tin (pan). Heat the butter and 1 tablespoon of the oil in a large frying pan. Fry the zucchini for 3–4 minutes, stirring frequently, until softened but not browned. Remove from the heat.

Bring the stock to the boil in a large pan. Sprinkle in the polenta, stirring with a wooden spoon, and continue to stir for 5 minutes, or until the polenta thickens and begins to come away from the sides of the pan. Remove from the heat and stir in the zucchini. Season to taste.

Tip the polenta into the roasting tin, spreading evenly, then sprinkle with Parmesan and leave for 1 hour to cool and set.

Heat a ridged frying pan over a high heat. Cut the polenta into slices, brush with the rest of the oil and cook for 2–4 minutes on each side, until golden. Alternatively, cook under a preheated grill (broiler).

PASTA and GNOCCHI

Chicken Cannelloni

2 tablespoons olive oil or
  butter, plus extra
1 onion, finely chopped
250 g (9 oz) ground (minced)
  chicken
250 g (9 oz) ground (minced)
  veal
2 tablespoons tomato paste
125 ml (4 fl oz/½ cup) water
salt and freshly ground black
  pepper
¼ teaspoon nutmeg
packet cannelloni tubes
375 ml (12 fl oz/1½ cups)
  bottled pasta sauce
125 ml (4 fl oz/½ cup) water
Parmesan, shaved, to serve

Béchamel Sauce

175 g (6 oz) butter
85 g (3 oz/¾ cup) plain (all-
  purpose) flour
1 litre (1¾ pints/4 cups) milk
⅛ teaspoon nutmeg
salt and freshly ground black
  pepper
3 tablespoons Parmesan,
  shaved
2 eggs, beaten

Serves 6

Preheat the oven to 180°C (350°F/Gas mark 4). Heat the oil or butter in a large frying pan, add the onion and sauté for 2 minutes. Add the chicken and veal and stir until browned. Add the tomato paste, water, salt and pepper, to taste, and nutmeg.

To make the béchamel sauce, melt the butter in a frying pan, add the flour and stir for 1 minute. Remove from the heat and gradually add the milk, stirring well. Return to the heat and stir until the sauce thickens and boils. Remove from the heat, stir in the nutmeg, seasonings, cheese and eggs. Remove ½ cup of sauce and stir it into the mince mixture.

Fill the cannelloni tubes with meat mixture. Grease a large ovenproof dish. Mix the pasta sauce and water together and spread half over the base of the dish. Place the filled cannelloni tubes in two rows in the dish then pour over the remaining pasta sauce. Pour over the béchamel sauce, spread evenly and sprinkle with a little grated Parmesan.

Dot with butter and bake for 30–35 minutes, or until golden brown. Serve hot.

Cannelloni Stuffed with Ricotta in Tomato Sauce

12 cannelloni tubes
340 g (12 oz) ricotta cheese
2 eggs
55 g (2 oz) Parmesan, shaved
salt and freshly ground black
  pepper, to taste
pinch of ground nutmeg
4–6 large ripe tomatoes,
  skinned and chopped
3 tablespoons olive oil
55 g (2 oz) butter

Serves 4–6

Preheat the oven to 180°C (350°F/Gas mark 4).

Cook the cannelloni tubes according to the packet instructions. Set aside until ready to fill.

In a bowl, thoroughly mix the ricotta cheese, eggs and half the Parmesan. Season with salt, pepper and nutmeg.

Place the tomatoes in a pan and cook, uncovered, until they are a thick pulp, stirring occasionally. Remove from the heat and stir in the oil gradually.

Drain the cannelloni and fill with ricotta cheese mixture. Place the filled cannelloni side by side in a single layer in a buttered shallow baking dish. Pour the tomato sauce around and over the cannelloni, sprinkle with the remaining Parmesan and dot with butter.

Bake for 20 minutes, or until the sauce is bubbling. Serve at once.

Fettuccine Alfredo

225 g (8 oz) fettuccine
115 g (4 oz) butter
115 g (4 oz) Parmesan, plus
   extra to garnish
salt and freshly ground black
   pepper
250 (8 fl oz/1 cup) single (light)
   cream
parsley, finely chopped, to
   garnish

Serves 6

Cook the fettucine in boiling salted water for 15 minutes, or until *al dente*.

Meanwhile, melt the butter in a large pan then add the Parmesan, salt, pepper and cream. Cook over a low heat, stirring constantly, until blended.

Drain the fettucine. Immediately add to the cheese mixture and toss until the pasta is well coated. Place in a heated serving dish, sprinkle with parsley and extra Parmesan and serve at once.

Fettuccine with Pesto Sauce

85 g (3 oz/1½ cups) fresh basil
   leaves
30 g (1 oz) pine nuts, toasted
2 garlic cloves, roughly
   chopped
3 tablespoons Parmesan, plus
   extra to garnish
3 tablespoons pecorino
   cheese, grated
125 ml (4 fl oz/½ cup) olive oil
salt and freshly ground
   pepper, to taste
365 g (13 oz) fettuccine
1 teaspoon salt

Serves 6

Place the basil, pine nuts, garlic, cheeses, oil and salt and pepper in a food processor. Process until well combined.

Cook the pasta in boiling salted water according to the packet instructions, until *al dente*. Strain in a colander, return to the pan, and toss with pesto sauce.

Serve with extra Parmesan.

Rigatoni with Pumpkin

450 g (1 lb) rigatoni
85 g (3 oz) butter
225 g (8 oz) pumpkin, cut into
  small cubes
1 tablespoon fresh chives,
  chopped
pinch of ground nutmeg
30 g (1 oz) Parmesan, shaved
freshly ground black pepper,
  to taste

Serves 4

Cook the rigatoni in a large pan of boiling salted water according to the packet instructions, or until *al dente*. Drain, set aside and keep warm.

Meanwhile, melt 55 g (2 oz) butter in a large pan and cook the pumpkin over a medium heat for 5–10 minutes, or until tender.

Stir the chives, nutmeg, Parmesan, black pepper, rigatoni and remaining butter into the pumpkin mixture and toss to combine.

Serve immediately.

Squid and Herb Spaghetti

500 g (1 lb 2 oz) squid tubes,
   cleaned and cut into rings
500 g (1 lb 2 oz) spaghetti or
   vermicelli
2 teaspoons olive oil
1 red onion, finely diced
1 garlic clove, crushed
4 Roma tomatoes, deseeded
   and diced
85 g (3 oz/½ cup) pitted
   Kalamata olives, rinsed and
   drained, sliced
60 ml (2 fl oz/¼ cup) chicken
   or fish stock
60 ml (2 fl oz/¼ cup) dry white
   wine
3 tablespoons chopped fresh
   cilantro (coriander)
3 tablespoons chopped fresh
   mint
freshly ground black pepper

Serves 4

Bring a large pan of water to the boil. Using a slotted spoon or wire basket, carefully lower the squid into the water. Cook for 5–10 seconds, or until it just turns white and is firm. Drain. Plunge into iced water. Drain again. Set aside.

Bring a large pan of fresh, salted water to the boil. Add the pasta and cook until tender but still firm to the bite. Drain.

Meanwhile, place the oil, onion and garlic in a non-stick frying pan over a medium heat. Cook, stirring, for 3–4 minutes, or until the onion is soft. Add tomatoes, olives, bouillon and wine. Bring to a simmer. Simmer for 5 minutes. Stir in the cilantro, mint, squid and pepper, to taste. Cook for 1–2 minutes, or until heated through.

Drain the pasta. Add the squid mixture. Toss to combine.

Umbrian Chilli Garlic Spaghetti

500 g (1 lb 2 oz) spaghetti
125 ml (4 fl oz/½ cup) extra
   virgin olive oil
1 garlic clove, thinly sliced
1½ tablespoons green chilli,
   freshly chopped and
   deseeded
1 teaspoon fresh ginger,
   chopped
salt and freshly ground black
   pepper
15 g (½ oz) fresh Italian flat-
   leaf parsley, finely chopped
1 tablespoon lemon juice

Serves 4

Bring a large pan of salted water to the boil and add the spaghetti and a drop of oil to stop the pasta sticking. Bring back to the boil and then cook according to the packet instructions until *al dente*.

In a heavy frying pan set over medium heat, heat the rest of the oil, then add the garlic, chilli, ginger, salt and pepper, to taste, and cook until the garlic starts to turn golden

Add the parsley and lemon juice, reduce the heat and keep warm until the spaghetti is ready.

Strain the pasta and add it to the pan of sauce and toss to combine.

Penne Napolitana

450 g (1 lb) penne
salt
Parmesan, to serve

Napolitana Sauce
2 teaspoons olive oil
2 onions, chopped
2 garlic cloves, crushed
2 x 400 g (14 oz) cans
   tomatoes, undrained and
   mashed
175 ml (6 fl oz/¾ cup) red wine
1 tablespoon Italian flat leaf
   parsley, chopped
1 tablespoon fresh oregano,
   chopped or ½ teaspoon
   dried oregano
freshly ground black pepper,
   to taste

Serves 4

Cook the pasta in a large pan of boiling salted water for 15 minutes or according to the packet instructions until *al dente*.

Meanwhile, to make the Napolitana sauce, heat the oil in a frying pan set over a medium heat. Add the onions and garlic and cook, stirring, for 3 minutes, or until onions have softened.

Stir in the tomatoes, wine, parsley, oregano and black pepper to taste. Bring to a simmer and cook for 15 minutes, or until the sauce reduces and thickens.

To serve, spoon the sauce over the hot pasta and top with shavings of Parmesan.

Penne with Rocket, Hot Pancetta and Semi-Dried Tomatoes

450 g (1 lb) penne

salt

1 tablespoon extra virgin olive oil

2 garlic cloves, crushed

100 g (3½ oz) spicy pancetta, roughly chopped

250 ml (8 fl oz/1 cup) Italian Tomato Sauce (see recipe page 173)

100 g (3½ oz) semi-dried tomatoes

1 bunch rocket (arugula), washed and drained

salt and freshly ground black pepper, to taste

Parmesan, shaved, to serve

Serves 4

Cook the pasta in boiling salted water until *al dente* or according to the packet instructions. Drain and set aside.

Near the end of the cooking time, heat the oil in a frying pan set over medium heat and add the garlic and pancetta. Fry for 2 minutes, or until the garlic softens.

Add the cooked pasta, the Italian Tomato Sauce, semi-dried tomatoes, rocket, and salt and freshly ground pepper to the pan, and heat through.

Serve with shavings of Parmesan.

Penne Primavera

55 g (2 oz) butter

85 g (3 oz/3 cups) baby
   spinach

225 g (8 oz/2 cups) fresh
   shelled peas

280 g (10 oz/2 cups) shelled
   fava (broad) beans

4 tablespoons crème fraîche

1 bunch spring onions
   (scallions), finely sliced

2 tablespoons finely chopped
   fresh parsley

salt and freshly ground black
   pepper

6 tablespoons Parmesan,
   grated

300 g (10½ oz/3½ cups)
   penne

Serves 4

Melt the butter in a frying pan, add the spinach, cover and cook for 5 minutes, or until the leaves wilt. Set aside to cool.

Cook the peas and beans in a little boiling salted water for 5 minutes, or until tender, then drain.

Blend the spinach and crème fraîche to a purée in a food processor or with a hand blender. Return the purée to the pan and stir in the peas and beans. Mix in the scallions and parsley, season well and add half the Parmesan. Keep warm over a low heat.

Meanwhile, cook the pasta in boiling salted water until tender but still firm to the bite. Drain, then toss with the spinach sauce. Serve with the remaining Parmesan.

NOTE: You can use any lightly cooked vegetables or pasta shapes in this dish, but the green shades of peas, spinach, parsley and beans are particularly pretty.

Penne with Pancetta and Tomatoes

4 tablespoons extra virgin
   olive oil

200 g (7 oz) unsmoked
   pancetta or rindless lean
   bacon, roughly chopped

1 teaspoon crushed dried
   chillies

100 ml (3½ fl oz) dry white
   wine

1 sweet or mild onion, very
   finely chopped

salt

400 g (14 oz) can chopped
   tomatoes

400 g (14 oz) penne

90 g (3 oz) Parmesan, freshly
   grated

Serves 4

Heat 2 tablespoons of the oil in a large, heavy skillet, then fry the pancetta or bacon and chillies for 2–3 minutes until the fat starts to run out. Add the wine and boil for 2–3 minutes, or until reduced by half.

Lower the heat, add the onion and ½ teaspoon of salt to the pancetta and cook, covered, for 8 minutes, stirring occasionally, until the onion has softened. Stir in the tomatoes and cook, covered, for 20–25 minutes or until thickened. If the mixture is a little dry, add 2 tablespoons of hot water. Season if necessary.

Meanwhile, cook the pasta in plenty of boiling salted water until tender but still firm to the bite. Drain, then transfer to a warmed serving bowl. Stir in the remaining oil and half the sauce. Mix, then add 4 tablespoons of Parmesan. Toss, then spoon over the rest of the sauce and serve with the remaining Parmesan.

Ravioli

1 quantity Italian Tomato
   Sauce (see recipe page 173)
Parmesan or romano cheese,
   grated (shredded), to
   garnish

Pasta Dough

1 tablespoon salt
3 tablespoons olive oil
5 eggs
340 g (12 oz) plain (all-
   purpose) flour

Filling

2 tablespoons olive oil
340 g (12 oz) minced (ground)
   beef or shredded chicken
225 g (8 oz) fresh spinach,
   cooked
2 eggs, beaten
1 tablespoon Parmesan,
   shaved
salt and freshly ground black
   pepper

Serves 6

To make the pasta dough, combine the salt, olive oil, and eggs in a food processor. Gradually add the flour, pulsing to mix. The dough is ready when it clings together and feels springy.

To make the filling, heat the oil in a frying pan. Add the meat and cook until browned, then place in a bowl. Finely chop the spinach and mix with the meat. Add the eggs, Parmesan, salt and pepper. Mix well. Set aside until ready to use.

Divide the pasta dough into quarters. Roll each quarter into a rectangle that is 3 mm (1/8 in) thick. Cut the dough lengthways (using a pastry cutter, if you have one) into strips 12 cm (5 in) wide.

Place 2 teaspoons of filling in the centre of one half of the pastry every 8.5 cm (3½ in), then fold over the other half covering the filling. Seal the whole strip by pressing the long edges together with the prongs of a fork.

Press the two layers of dough together between the mounds of filling and cut in the middle between the mounds with the pastry cutter, again sealing the cut edges with the prongs of a fork.

Bring a large pan of salted water to the boil. Add the ravioli about one third at a time. Cook for 20 minutes, or until tender. Remove with a slotted spoon. Drain well.

Serve topped with heated Italian Tomato Sauce and sprinkled with Parmesan or romano cheese.

Pork and Sage Ravioli

1 quantity Italian Tomato
  Sauce (see recipe page
  173), to serve
fresh Parmesan shavings, to
  serve

Pasta Dough
1 tablespoon salt
3 tablespoons olive oil
5 eggs
340 g (12 oz) plain (all-
  purpose) flour

Pork and Sage Filling
280 g (10 oz) ricotta cheese,
  drained
55 g (2 oz) lean bacon, finely
  chopped
150 g (5 oz) lean cooked pork,
  finely diced
1 teaspoon fresh parsley,
  finely chopped
½ teaspoon fresh sage, finely
  chopped
1 teaspoon Parmesan
  shavings
grated nutmeg, to taste
freshly ground black pepper,
  to taste

To make the pasta dough, combine the salt, olive oil, and eggs in a food processor. Gradually add the flour, pulsing to mix. The dough is ready when it clings together and feels springy.

To make the pork and sage filling, in a bowl, mix the ricotta cheese, bacon, pork, parsley, sage and Parmesan. Season with nutmeg and black pepper. Cover and set aside while making the pasta.

Divide the pasta dough into quarters. Roll each quarter into a rectangle 3 mm (1/8 in) thick. Cut the dough lengthways (using a pastry cutter, if you have one) into strips 12 cm (5 in) wide.

Place 2 teaspoons of filling in the centre of one half of the pastry every 8.5 cm (3½ in), then fold over the other half covering the filling. Seal the whole strip by pressing the long edges together with the prongs of a fork.

Press the two layers of dough together between the mounds of filling and cut in the middle between the mounds with the pastry cutter, again sealing the cut edges with the prongs of a fork.

Add the ravioli gradually, about a third at a time, to a large pan of rapidly boiling, salted water. Cook for 20 minutes, or until tender. Remove with a slotted spoon. Drain well.

Serve topped with heated Italian Tomato Sauce and sprinkled with Parmesan.

Serves 6

Tagliatelle with Bolognese Sauce

3 tablespoons olive oil

2 tablespoons butter

125 g (4½ oz) unsmoked
  pancetta or rindless bacon,
  roughly chopped

1 small onion, very finely
  chopped

1 small carrot, very finely
  chopped

1 stick celery, very finely
  chopped

1 small garlic clove, crushed

1 lb (450 g) ground (minced)
  beef steak

125 ml (4 fl oz/½ cup) dry
  white wine

2 tablespoons tomato paste

125 ml (4 fl oz/½ cup) beef
  bouillon

salt and freshly ground black
  pepper

125 ml (4 fl oz/½ cup) full-fat
  (whole) milk

1 lb (450 g) fresh tagliatelle

Parmesan, shavings, to serve

Serves 4

Heat the oil and butter in a large heavy pan set over low heat. When sizzling add the pancetta or bacon, onion, carrot, celery and garlic and cook for 5–7 minutes, until the vegetables have softened. Stir from time to time. Add the beef and cook, stirring constantly for 3–5 minutes, or until browned.

Pour in the wine and boil for 2–3 minutes, or until reduced by more than half. Mix in the tomato paste, bouillon and seasoning. Return to the boil, then simmer very gently, uncovered, for 2–2½ hours, stirring from time to time. Add 2 tablespoons of milk whenever the sauce starts to dry out.

Cook the pasta in plenty of boiling salted water until tender but still firm to the bite. Drain, then transfer one-third of the pasta to a warmed serving bowl and spoon over 1 tablespoon of the sauce. Repeat, then add the remaining pasta and toss well. Spoon over the remaining sauce. Serve with the Parmesan.

Tagliatelle with Creamy Seafood Sauce

400 g (14 oz) tagliatelle

250 ml (8 fl oz/1 cup) chicken
   stock

450 g (1 lb) marinara mix
   (mussels, fish, shrimp
   (prawns), oysters, squid,
   washed

25 g (¾ oz) butter

1 onion, finely chopped

3 tablespoons plain (all-
   purpose) flour

225 g (8 oz) sour cream

2 tablespoons fresh parsley,
   chopped

Serves 4

Cook the pasta in a large pan of boiling salted water according to the packet instructions until *al dente*. Drain well.

Meanwhile, heat the stock in a deep pan and poach the seafood mix until cooked. Drain, reserving the liquid.

Melt the butter in a frying pan and sauté the onion for 5 minutes, or until translucent. Stir in the flour and cook until frothy. Pour in the fish poaching liquid and cook, stirring, until the sauce boils and thickens. Stir in the sour cream, parsley and seafood. Bring to the boiling point, but do not boil. Serve over cooked pasta.

Tagliatelle with Walnuts and Blue Cheese

200 g (7 oz) tagliatelle

3 tablespoon olive oil

150 g (5 oz/1 cup) walnut pieces

100 g (3½ oz) blue cheese

fresh chives, chopped, to garnish

Serves 2

Cook the pasta in a large pan of boiling salted water according to the packet instructions or until *al dente*. Drain well.

Meanwhile, heat the oil in a frying pan and cook the walnuts for 5 minutes, or until golden and toasted. Pour the oil and walnut mixture over the pasta and toss to coat. Crumble over the cheese. Garnish with chives and serve.

Tagliatelle and Meatballs with Spicy Tomato Sauce

55 g (2 oz/1 cup) fresh
breadcrumbs, made from
2 slices stonebaked white
loaf, crusts removed

450 g (1 lb) ground (minced)
beef

15 g (4 oz/½ cup) finely
chopped bacon

1 small onion, finely chopped

3 tablespoons fresh parsley,
chopped, plus extra to
garnish

1 egg, beaten

salt and freshly ground black
pepper

2 tablespoons sunflower oil

500 ml (17 fl oz/2 cups) spicy
roasted garlic pasta sauce

450 g (1 lb) tagliatelle

Serves 4

Place the breadcrumbs in a large bowl and combine with the ground beef, bacon, onion, parsley, egg and seasoning and mix well. Shape the mixture into 20 balls, and then flatten slightly with the palm of your hand. Refrigerate for 10 minutes.

Heat the oil in a large skillet and over a medium-high heat, brown the meatballs on all sides for about 5 minutes (you may need to do this in 2 batches). Spoon off any excess oil from the skillet and pour the pasta sauce over the meatballs in the pan. Reduce the heat to medium and simmer gently for 10 minutes, turning the meatballs occasionally, until cooked through.

Meanwhile, cook the pasta in plenty of boiling salted water until tender but still firm to the bite, then drain. Serve the meatballs with the pasta and garnish with the extra parsley.

Lasagne

2 tablespoons olive oil

225 g (8 oz) minced (ground)
    beef

225 g (8 oz) lean minced
    (ground) pork

1 onion, finely chopped

1 glove garlic, finely chopped

1 teaspoon fresh parsley,
    chopped

225 g (8 oz) tomato paste

500 ml (17 fl oz/2 cups) water

salt and freshly ground black
    pepper

225 (8 oz) lasagne sheets

30 g (1 oz) mozzarella cheese,
    sliced thinly

225 g (8 oz) ricotta cheese,
    crumbed

2 tablespoons romano
    cheese, grated

Serves 4–6

Heat the oil in frying pan, add the beef, pork, onion, garlic and parsley and heat until the meat is browned. Stir in the tomato paste, water, salt and pepper and simmer, uncovered, for 1½ hours.

Preheat the oven to 180°C (350°F/Gas mark 4).

Bring a large pan of water to the boil, add 1½ teaspoons salt and the lasagne sheets.

In a large, shallow, rectangular baking dish, arrange alternate layers of lasagne sheets, sauce, mozzarella and ricotta cheese. Repeat the layers until the lasagne sheets and sauce and two cheeses are all used, ending with ricotta cheese.

Sprinkle with grated romano cheese and bake for 25–30 minutes. Allow to stand for 10 minutes before serving.

Seafood Lasagne

2 tablespoons olive oil

1 leek, white part only, finely chopped

400 g (14 oz) can diced tomatoes

2 tablespoons tomato paste

450 g (1 lb) uncooked shrimp (prawns), shelled and deveined, cut into small pieces

225 g (8 oz) boneless white fish fillets, cut into small pieces

15 sheets spinach lasagne

115 g (4 oz) mozzarella, thinly sliced

Serves 4

Preheat the oven to 180°C (350°F/Gas mark 4).

Heat the oil in a large frying pan, add the leek and cook until tender. Stir in the tomatoes and tomato paste. Cook until the mixture boils then simmer uncovered until the sauce is slightly thickened. Stir in the shrimp and fish pieces, cover, and cook over low heat for about 5 minutes.

Spoon one-third of the sauce into the bottom of a 5 cm (2 in) deep casserole dish. Arrange the lasagne sheets in a single layer over the seafood sauce. Spoon another third of the sauce over the lasagne, and top with another layer of lasagne.

Spread the remaining third of sauce over the lasagne and top with mozzarella cheese. Bake in the oven for 40 minutes.

Spaghetti Marinara

60 ml (2 fl oz/¼ cup) olive oil

900 g (2 lb) marinara mix
(oysters, scallops, shrimp
(prawns), calamari, fish
fillet pieces), washed and
drained

2 garlic cloves, sliced

2 x 400 g (14 oz) cans
tomatoes, puréed

1½ teaspoons salt

1 teaspoon fresh oregano

1 teaspoon fresh parsley,
chopped

¼ teaspoon freshly ground
black pepper

2 tablespoons red wine
(optional)

340 g (12 oz) spaghetti

Serves 6–8

Heat the oil in a large frying pan and sauté the marinara mix over a medium heat for 5 minutes. Remove from the pan and keep warm. Add the garlic to the pan and sauté until golden.

Stir in the tomatoes, salt, oregano, parsley, pepper and wine (if using). Cook rapidly, uncovered, for 15 minutes, or until the sauce has thickened. Stir occasionally. If the sauce becomes too thick, add ¼–½ cup (2–4 fl oz) water. Add the marinara mix and reheat gently.

Meanwhile, cook the spaghetti in a large pan of boiling, salted water for 15 minutes or until *al dente*. Drain.

Serve immediately with marinara sauce poured on top.

Spaghetti Carbonara

225–340 g (8–12 oz) fettucine

2 tablespoons olive oil

3 slices bacon, finely diced

2 eggs

45 g (1½ oz) Parmesan, grated

250 ml (8 fl oz/1 cup) single (light) cream

salt and freshly ground black pepper, to taste

Serves 4

Bring a large pan of boiling salted water to the boil. Add the fettucine and cook for 8 minutes, or according to packet instructions until *al dente*.

Just before the fettucine is ready, heat the oil in a frying pan and fry the bacon.

In a bowl, beat the eggs and cheese together.

Drain the pasta and return it to the hot pan. Add the egg and cheese mixture, cream, plenty of black pepper and crisp bacon. Mix well. Place the pan over a low heat for a minute or so, stirring constantly.

Place in a hot dish and serve immediately.

Tuna-Filled Shells

16 giant pasta shells
(conchiglioni)

Tuna Filling
225 g (8 oz) ricotta cheese,
drained
400 g (14 oz) can tuna in
brine, drained and flaked
½ red bell pepper (capsicum),
diced
1 tablespoon capers,
chopped
1 teaspoon fresh chives,
snipped
4 tablespoons Swiss cheese,
grated (shredded)
pinch of ground nutmeg
freshly ground black pepper,
to taste
2 tablespoons Parmesan
shavings

Makes 16

Cook 8 pasta shells in a large pan of boiling salted water for 15 minutes or until *al dente*. Drain, rinse under cold running water, and drain again. Set aside, then repeat with remaining shells, ensuring the cooked shells do not overlap.

To make the tuna filling, put the ricotta and tuna in a bowl and mix to combine. Mix in the red capsicum, capers, chives and 2 tablespoons Swiss cheese, nutmeg and black pepper to taste.

Fill each shell with ricotta mixture, and place in a lightly greased, shallow ovenproof dish. Sprinkle with Parmesan and the remaining Swiss cheese. Place under a preheated grill (broiler) and cook until the cheese melts.

Gnocchi with Spinach, Green Peas and Ricotta

200 g (7 oz) fresh spinach
    leaves
200 g (7 oz) fresh or frozen
    green peas, shelled
200 g (7 oz) ricotta, drained
freshly ground black pepper
ground nutmeg
55 g (2 oz) butter
2 eggs, lightly beaten
3 tablespoons dried
    breadcrumbs
5 tablespoons plain (all-
    purpose) flour
90 g (3 oz) Parmesan shavings

Serves 4

Steam the spinach in a steamer set over a pan of boiling water until tender. Drain and squeeze to remove the excess liquid. Set aside and when cool tip into the bowl of a food processor.

In another pan, cook the peas in a pan of boiling water until tender. Drain and add to the spinach, then pulse to process.

Place the spinach mixture and ricotta in a pan. Season to taste with black pepper and nutmeg. Add 15 g (½ oz) butter and cook over a very low heat, stirring frequently until the butter melts and all the excess liquid evaporates.

Remove from the heat. Beat in the eggs, then add the breadcrumbs, flour and half the Parmesan. The mixture should be firm enough to hold its shape, but soft enough to create a light-textured gnocchi.

Using well-floured hands, take heaped spoonfuls of mixture and roll lightly into small ovals. Bring a large pan of water to the boil, then reduce the heat.

Drop the gnocchi in a few at a time and cook for 4–5 minutes, or until they rise to the surface. Remove from the pan and drain. Cover and keep warm.

Melt the remaining butter in a pan and cook until lightly browned. Pour butter over the gnocchi, sprinkle with the remaining Parmesan and serve.

Gnocchi

3 medium potatoes, washed
115 g (4 oz) plain (all-purpose)
  flour, sifted, plus extra
1 egg, beaten
salt
extra flour
oil
Italian Tomato Sauce (see
  recipe page 173) or
  Bolognese Sauce (see
  recipe page 154)
Parmesan shavings, to
  garnish

Serves 4

Boil unpeeled potatoes until tender. Peel while hot and place in a mixing bowl. Mash the potatoes straight away, adding sifted the flour, a little at a time, while the potatoes are still hot. Add the egg and salt and beat until smooth.

Turn out onto a well-floured work surface. Knead, working in enough flour to form a smooth, soft, non-sticky dough. Roll each the dough to pencil thickness. Cut into 2 cm (¾ in) squares. With the tines of a floured fork, press each piece so that it curls. Place on waxed paper. Sprinkle lightly with flour.

Add the gnocchi a little at a time to a large pan of rapidly boiling salted water with a little oil added. Cook for about 5 minutes, or until the gnocchi comes to the surface. Drain and keep warm in a heated bowl until all the gnocchi is cooked.

Serve with Italian Tomato Sauce or Bolognese Sauce, sprinkled with Parmesan.

Tricolor Gnocchi with Fresh Herbs

300 g (10½ oz) tricolor
  gnocchi
salt
100 g (3½ oz) butter
1 garlic clove, chopped
2 tablespoons fresh thyme
2 tablespoons chopped fresh
  parsley
1 teaspoon fresh oregano
1 bunch fresh basil, chopped
1 red bell pepper (capsicum),
  seeds removed and sliced
  into thin strips
Parmesan cheese, shavings,
  to serve
6 sun-dried tomatoes, finely
  sliced, to garnish

Serves 4

Bring a large pan of boiling salted water to the boil, add the gnocchi then when they rise to the surface remove each with a slotted spoon, drain and transfer to a plate.

Melt the butter in a skillet. Add the garlic and herbs and fry for 1 minute on high heat, shaking the pan continuously. Add the gnocchi and bell pepper and sauté until the gnocchi are golden brown and well coated with herbs.

Serve with Parmesan shavings and slices of sun-dried tomatoes.

Gnocchi with Gorgonzola Sauce

3 medium potatoes, washed
115 g (4 oz) plain (all-purpose),
    flour, sifted, plus extra for
    dusting
1 egg
salt
oil
Parmesan shavings, to
    garnish

Gorgonzola Sauce
200 g (7 oz) Gorgonzola or
    blue cheese, crumbled
175 ml (6 fl oz/¾ cup) milk
55 g (2 oz) butter
55 g (2 oz) walnuts, toasted
    and chopped
175 ml (6 fl oz/¾ cup)
    thickened (double/heavy)
    cream
freshly ground black pepper,
    to taste

Serves 6

To make the Gorgonzola sauce, put the cheese, milk and butter in a pan and cook over low heat, stirring, for 4–5 minutes, or until the cheese melts. Stir in the walnuts, cream and black pepper. Bring to a simmer and cook for 5 minutes, or until the sauce reduces and thickens.

Boil the unpeeled potatoes until tender. Drain, then peel while hot and place in a mixing bowl. Mash the potatoes straight away, adding sifted flour, a little at a time, while the potatoes are still hot. Add the egg and 1 teaspoon salt and beat until smooth.

Turn the potato mixture onto a well-floured board and knead, working in enough flour to form a smooth, soft, non-sticky dough. Roll the dough to pencil thickness. Cut into 2 cm (¾ in) squares.

With the prongs of a floured fork, press each piece so that it curls. Place on waxed paper. Sprinkle lightly with flour.

Bring a large pan of salted water to the boil. Add a drop of oil to stop the pieces sticking together. Add the gnocchi a few at a time. Cook for about 5 minutes, or until the gnocchi rise to the surface. Drain and keep warm in a heated bowl until all the gnocchi is cooked.

Spoon Gorgonzola sauce over the hot gnocchi and toss to combine.

Gnocchi with Italian Tomato Sauce

3 medium potatoes, washed
115 g (4 oz) plain (all-purpose)
    flour, sifted, plus extra for
    dusting
1 egg
salt
Parmesan shavings, to
    garnish

Italian Tomato Sauce

2 tablespoons olive oil
1 small onion, finely chopped
2 garlic cloves, crushed
900 g (2 lb) tomatoes,
    skinned, seeded and
    chopped, or 2 x 400 g
    (14 oz) cans whole
    tomatoes, diced
salt and freshly ground black
    pepper
½ teaspoon caster (superfine)
    sugar
15 g (½ oz) fresh basil
1 sprig oregano
1 bay leaf
1 tablespoon tomato paste

Serves 4

To make the Italian Tomato Sauce, in a large pan, set over medium heat, heat the oil. Add the onion and garlic and fry for 5–6 minutes, stirring until the onion is translucent. Add the tomatoes and all the other ingredients and bring to the boil. Reduce the heat, cover, and simmer for 45 minutes, stirring occasionally.

Purée the sauce in a blender or food processor, if you like a smooth consistency.

Meanwhile, boil the unpeeled potatoes until tender. Peel while hot and place in a mixing bowl. Mash the potatoes straight away, adding sifted flour, a little at a time, while potatoes are still hot. Add the egg and 1 teaspoon salt and beat until smooth.

Turn the potato mixture out onto a well-floured board and knead, working in enough flour to form a smooth, soft, non-sticky dough. Roll out to pencil thickness. Cut into 2 cm (¾ in) pieces. Cut into 2 cm (¾ in) squares.

With the prongs of a floured fork, press each piece so that it curls. Place on waxed paper. Sprinkle lightly with flour.

Bring a large pan of salted water to the boil. Add a drop of oil to stop the pieces sticking together. Add the gnocchi a few at a time. Cook for about 5 minutes, or until the gnocchi rise to the surface. Drain and keep warm in a heated bowl until all the gnocchi is cooked.

Spoon the Italian tomato sauce over the hot gnocchi and toss to combine.

Gnocchi with Spinach, Rocket and Basil Pesto

450 g (1 lb) fresh potato
 gnocchi
salt
55 g (2 oz/2 cups) baby
 spinach leaves, washed
55 g (2 oz/2 cups) baby
 arugula (rocket) leaves,
 washed
30 g/1 oz/1 cup fresh basil
 leaves
2 garlic cloves
4 tablespoons pine nuts,
 toasted
40 g/1¼ oz/¼ cup Parmesan
 shavings, plus extra, to
 garnish
2 tablespoons extra virgin
 olive oil
freshly ground black pepper

Serves 4

Cook the gnocchi in a large pan of rapidly boiling salted water, just until they float to the surface. Remove with a slotted spoon, drain well and set aside. Keep warm.

Steam the spinach until it wilts in a steamer set over a pan of simmering water. Drain and squeeze out any excess moisture.

Put the spinach, arugula, basil, garlic, pine nuts and Parmesan in a food processor and process until smooth. With the motor running, gradually add the oil and process to form a smooth paste.

Spoon the pesto over the cooked gnocchi and toss to coat. Season with the pepper. Serve with Parmesan.

FISH and SEAFOOD

Devilled Whitebait

sunflower or peanut oil, for
deep-frying
5 tablespoons plain (all-
purpose) flour
salt and freshly ground black
pepper
½ teaspoon cayenne pepper
1 teaspoon ground coriander
400 g (14 oz) frozen whitebait,
defrosted, rinsed and dried
15 g (½ oz/½ cup) flat-leaf
parsley
lemon wedges, to serve

Serves 4

Heat the oil in a deep heavy pan.

Meanwhile, place the flour in a large plastic bag and add
½ teaspoon of salt, black pepper, the cayenne pepper and
coriander. Shake to mix, then add the whitebait to the bag a few
at a time and shake gently to coat.

Fry the whitebait in batches for 4–5 minutes, until crisp and
golden, then drain on absorbent paper. Fry the parsley for
30–45 seconds, taking care as the oil will spit, then drain on
absorbent paper. Sprinkle the whitebait with salt and serve with
the deep-fried parsley and lemon wedges.

Cod with Basil Aïoli

1 garlic clove, crushed

2 tablespoons olive oil

1 tablespoon lemon juice

4 cod cutlets

1 quantity of Basil Aïoli (see recipe page 276)

1 quantity of Parmesan Potatoes (see recipe page 97)

Serves 4

Combine the garlic, olive oil and lemon juice in a non-metallic dish, and marinate the fish cutlets in it, covered in the refrigerator, for 1 hour.

Lightly oil a char-grill or pan, and grill (broil) the fish for 3 minutes on each side.

Serve with aïoli and Parmesan potatoes.

Fish with Basil Cream Sauce

4 fish fillets (whiting, trout,
   snapper, sea bass)

Basil Cream Sauce

3 tablespoons fresh basil,
   finely chopped
1 tablespoon lemon juice
1 tablespoon capers, drained
115 g (4 fl oz/½ cup) light sour
   cream

Serves 4

Grill, poach or steam the fish until the flesh flakes easily.

To make the basil cream sauce, mix the basil, lemon juice, capers and sour cream together until combined. Pour the sauce evenly over the fish fillets and serve.

Garlic and Lemon Mussels

2 tablespoons olive oil

1 kg (2¼ lb) mussels

6 garlic cloves, finely chopped

1 chilli, sliced

15 g/½ oz basil leaves, roughly
  chopped

4 Roma tomatoes, diced

250 ml (8 fl oz/1 cup) white
  wine

1 teaspoon salt

freshly ground black pepper

1 lemon, cut into wedges

Serves 4

Heat the oil in a heavy pan until almost smoking. Add the
mussels. They should make a popping sound when they hit the
oil. Cook for 1 minute.

Add the garlic, chilli, basil, tomatoes and white wine. Cover
with a lid and cook for another 4 minutes.

Discard any mussels that do not open during cooking. Season
with salt and pepper. Serve with lemon wedges.

Mussels with Tomatoes and Wine

1 kg (2¼ lb) fresh mussels,
  scrubbed and beards
  removed
1 French shallot, chopped
250 ml (8 fl oz/1 cup) dry white
  wine
15 g (½ oz) bunch fresh
  chives, chopped

**Tomato and Smoked
  Salmon Sauce**
2 teaspoons olive oil
2 garlic cloves, crushed
2 French shallots, chopped
3 slices smoked salmon,
  sliced into thin strips
1 red bell pepper (capsicum),
  seeded and sliced
1 tablespoon tomato paste
400 g (14 oz) can diced
  tomatoes
7 g (¼ oz/ ¼ cup) fresh
  parsley, chopped

Serves 4

For the tomato and smoked salmon sauce, heat the oil in a non-stick frying pan over a medium heat. Add the garlic and shallots. Cook, stirring, for 1–2 minutes. Add the salmon and bell pepper. Cook, stirring, for 3 minutes. Stir in the tomato paste. Cook for 3–4 minutes, or until it becomes deep red and develops a rich aroma. Add the tomatoes. Cook, stirring, for 5 minutes, or until the mixture starts to thicken. Stir in the parsley. Keep warm.

Meanwhile, place the mussels, shallot and wine in a large pan set over a high heat, discarding any mussels that are open. Cover. Bring to the boil then reduce the heat. Cook for 5 minutes or until the mussels open. Discard any mussels that do not open.

Add the sauce to the mussels. Toss to combine.

To serve, divide the mixture between deep bowls and scatter with chives. Accompany with crusty bread and a glass of red wine.

Olive and Herb Fish Steaks

2 tablespoons olive oil

2 onions, sliced

2 garlic cloves, finely chopped

225 g (8 oz) black olives,
    pitted

1½ teaspoons dried marjoram

375 ml (12 fl oz/1½ cups) white
    wine vinegar

salt and freshly ground black
    pepper, to taste

1 tablespoon olive oil, extra

4 fish steaks (whiting,
    trout, snapper, sea bass,
    haddock)

1 tablespoon fresh parsley,
    chopped

Serves 4

Heat the olive oil in a frying pan and sauté the onions and garlic until translucent. Add the olives, marjoram, vinegar, salt and pepper. Cook for 2–3 minutes.

In a separate frying pan, heat the extra olive oil and cook the fish steaks until just cooked through. The cooking time will depend on the thickness of the fish steak. The fish is cooked when the flesh is white. Serve topped with the olive mixture and garnished with parsley.

Garlic Shrimp

125 ml (4 fl oz/½ cup) olive oil

4 large garlic cloves, peeled

1 tablespoon fresh parsley, chopped

½ teaspoon salt

1 kg (2¼ lb) small green shrimp (prawns), peeled and deveined

Serves 12 as an appetiser, 8 as an entrée

In a bowl, combine the oil, garlic, parsley and salt. Add the shrimp and let stand for 2 hours covered in the refrigerator.

Preheat the oven to 240°C (475°F/Gas mark 9). Place the shrimp and marinade in an ovenproof casserole dish and bake for 10 minutes, or until the shrimp turn pink. Remove the garlic cloves.

Serve as an appetiser on small cocktail sticks, or as an entrée in small ramekins.

Shrimp in Tomato Sauce

55 g (2 oz) butter

1 large onion, finely chopped

1 garlic clove, crushed

4 large tomatoes, skinned and
   chopped

1 tablespoon tomato paste

500 ml (17 fl oz/2 cups) dry
   white wine

1 bay leaf

salt and freshly ground black
   pepper, to taste

900 g (2 lb) shrimp (prawns),
   cooked and shelled

6 spring onions (scallions),
   chopped

Serves 4

Heat the butter in a pan set over medium heat. Add the onion
and garlic and cook until the onion is soft. Add the tomatoes,
tomato paste, wine and bay leaf. Season with salt and pepper.
Bring to the boil, reduce the heat and simmer, uncovered, for
30 minutes, or until the sauce is reduced and thickened.
Remove the bay leaf.

Add the shrimp and spring onions, and simmer gently until the
shrimp are heated through.

Shrimp with Rosemary and Garlic

450 g (1 lb) shrimp (prawns)

2 garlic cloves, crushed

3 tablespoons olive oil

¼ teaspoon freshly ground
  black pepper

2 sprigs rosemary

3 tablespoons butter

125 ml (4 fl oz/½ cup) dry
  vermouth

Serves 4

In a large bowl, combine the shrimp, garlic, olive oil, pepper and rosemary. Toss well to combine. Cover with plastic wrap (cling film) and allow to marinate in the refrigerator for 8 hours or overnight.

In a large frying pan, melt the butter over high heat, add the shrimp and marinade and sauté until pink, about 2 minutes.

Transfer the shrimp to a bowl with a slotted spoon. Discard the rosemary the sprigs.

Pour the vermouth into a frying pan, bring to the boil and reduce to a moderately thick consistency.

Return the shrimp to the sauce and toss in the glaze. Spoon the shrimp into a serving dish. Serve immediately.

Calamari with Garlic and Capers

1 carrot, peeled and chopped
1 onion, chopped
½ bunch thyme
8 garlic cloves
juice and zest of 1 lemon
100g (3½ oz) capers
4 calamari tubes

Marinade
1 teaspoon cumin
175 ml (6 fl oz/¾ cup) extra
    virgin olive oil
juice of 2 lemons
1 teaspoon salt
½ teaspoon ground black
    pepper
8 sprigs lemon thyme

Salad
2 heads radicchio
1 endive
2 teaspoons capers
½ cup flat-leaf parsley,
    chopped

Serves 4

Place the carrot, onion, thyme, garlic, lemon juice and zest, capers and 1 litre (1¾ pints/4 cups) water in a pan, bring to the boil and simmer for 10 minutes.

Clean the calamari tubes under running water. Place into the simmering poaching liquid for approximately 2 minutes.

Remove the garlic cloves from the poaching liquid and slice.

Place the ingredients for the marinade in a bowl, add the sliced garlic and mix together.

Remove the calamari from the poaching liquid and cut into 5 cm (2 in) wide strips. Place into the marinade and leave in the refrigerator for 30 minutes.

Wash the radicchio and endive, discard the outer leaves, place in a bowl and mix with the capers and parsley.

Remove the calamari from the marinade and add to the salad. Use 60 ml (2 fl oz/¼ cup) of the marinade as a dressing. Serve immediately.

Calamari with Lemon and Herbs

75 ml (2 fl oz (1/3 cup) lemon
    juice
3 garlic cloves, crushed
125 ml (4 fl oz/1/2 cup) olive oil,
    plus 1 tablespoon extra
1 kg (2¼ lb) calamari, cut into
    thin rings

Dressing

75 ml (2 fl oz (1/3 cup) lemon
    juice
75 ml (2 fl oz (1/3 cup) olive oil
7 g (¼ oz/ ¼ cup) parsley,
    chopped
1 garlic clove, crushed
1 teaspoon Dijon mustard
salt and freshly ground black
    pepper

Serves 4

Place the lemon juice, garlic and oil in a bowl, stir to combine then add the calamari and marinate for at least 3 hours. If time permits, marinate overnight.

To make the dressing, place all the ingredients in a bowl or screw-top jar and whisk or shake well until the dressing thickens slightly.

Heat the tablespoon of oil in a pan, add the calamari, and cook for a few minutes until cooked through. Alternatively, the calamari can be cooked on a char-grill plate.

Serve the calamari with lemon and herb dressing drizzled over.

Quick Fish Stew

oil, for greasing

450 g (1 lb) white fish
   (snapper, cod), diced

225 g (8 oz) marinara mix
   (mussels, prawns (shrimp),
   scallops, oysters, calamari)

2 onions, sliced

salt and freshly ground black
   pepper, to taste

400 g (14 oz) can diced
   tomatoes

125 ml (4 fl oz/½ cup) white
   wine or lemon juice

1 teaspoon dried oregano

1 tablespoon fresh parsley,
   chopped

Serves 4–6

Layer a portion of fish, marinara mix and onions in a greased baking dish suitable for cooking on a stovetop or pan. Season with salt and pepper. Cover the onions with tomatoes, pouring over some of the tomato juice from the can. Repeat the layers until all the fish, marinara mix, onions and tomatoes are used up.

Mix the wine, oregano and parsley together and pour over the seafood. Cook, uncovered, over a low heat for 25–30 minutes. Serve with crusty bread.

Snapper Fillets with White Wine and Parsley

55 g (2 oz/½ cup) plain (all-purpose) flour

1 teaspoon coarse ground pepper

¼ teaspoon sea salt

2 tablespoons olive oil

4 x 200 g (7 oz) snapper fillets

55 g (2 oz) butter

2 garlic cloves, crushed

125 ml (4 fl oz/½ cup) white wine

2 tablespoons fresh parsley, finely chopped

Serves 4

Combine the flour, pepper and salt in a dish, and coat the fish fillets evenly with flour, shaking off the excess.

Heat the oil in a pan, add the fish, and cook over a medium heat for 5–6 minutes on each side, depending on the thickness of the fish. Set the fish aside, and keep it warm.

Wipe out the pan, then melt the butter, add the garlic, and cook for 2 minutes. Add white wine and simmer, until the sauce reduces.

Just before serving, add the parsley to the sauce and serve with the fish.

Sardine Fritters with Minted Chilli Butter

12 fresh sardine fillets

4 tablespoons plain (all-
purpose) flour

1 egg blended with
2 tablespoons milk

115 g (4 oz) dried
breadcrumbs

oil, for cooking

Minted Chilli Butter

115 g (4 oz) butter, softened

3 tablespoons fresh mint,
finely chopped

2 spring onions (scallions),
finely chopped

1 garlic clove, crushed

¼ teaspoon red chilli,
chopped

freshly ground black pepper,
to taste

Serves 4

Coat the sardines in flour, dip in the egg and milk mixture, then coat with breadcrumbs.

To make minted chilli butter, place the butter, mint, spring onions, garlic, chilli and pepper in a bowl and mix well. Place the butter mixture on a piece of plastic wrap (cling film) and roll into a log. Refrigerate until required.

Heat the oil and one-third of the minted chilli butter in a large frying pan and cook the sardines for 1–2 minutes each side, or until golden. Serve the sardines topped with a slice of minted chilli butter.

Pan-Fried Sardines with Mixed Herbs

⅓ cup (1½ oz) plain (all-purpose) flour

3 tablespoons mixed herbs (parsley, basil, oregano and marjoram), roughly chopped

½ teaspoon coarse black pepper

pinch of sea salt

1.5 kg (3¼ lb) sardine fillets

60 ml (2 fl oz/¼ cup) olive oil

2 lemons, cut into wedges

Serves 4

On a large plate, combine the flour, herbs, pepper and salt.

Coat the sardine fillets with the flour mixture, pressing the mixture firmly onto fish.

Heat oil in a large frying pan, add sardines four at a time, and cook for 1–2 minutes on each side, or until they are crisp and lightly browned. Serve with lemon wedges.

Grilled Sardines

12 sardines, cleaned
60 ml (2 fl oz/¼ cup) extra
  virgin olive oil
sea salt
1 lemon, cut into wedges

Salad
1 green bell pepper
  (capsicum)
1 yellow bell pepper
  (capsicum)
3 tomatoes, diced
1 red onion, diced
2 tablespoons extra virgin
olive oil
1 tablespoon white wine
  vinegar
½ teaspoon sugar
salt and freshly ground black
  pepper

Serves 4

Place the sardines in a large shallow ceramic dish. Drizzle with olive oil and sprinkle over the salt, cover with cling film (plastic wrap) and refrigerate for 1–2 hours.

Preheat a grill (broiler) or barbecue. Cook the sardines for 3–4 minutes on each side, or until golden and cooked.

To make the salad, cut each green and yellow capsicum into four and remove the seeds.

Place on a baking tray under a hot grill (broiler) for 6–8 minutes, or until the skin blisters. Leave to cool, then remove the skin and dice the flesh. Toss together the capsicum, tomatoes, onion, olive oil, vinegar, sugar, salt and pepper.

Serve the sardines with lemon wedges and the salad.

Tonno al Forno

200 g (7 oz/1 cup) long grain
rice

1 tablespoon olive oil, plus
extra for greasing

½ large onion, finely diced

1 garlic clove, crushed

250 ml (8 fl oz/1 cup) double
(heavy) cream

250 ml (8 fl oz/1 cup)
tomato pasta sauce (from
supermarket)

75 g (2½ oz/½ cup) semi-dried
tomatoes, chopped

185 g (6½ oz) can tuna

4 spring onions (scallions),
chopped

7 g (¼ oz/¼ cup) basil, finely
chopped

50 g (1¾ oz) provolone
cheese, diced, plus 100 g
(3½ oz) grated (shredded)

salt and freshly ground black
pepper

Serves 4

Preheat oven to 200°C (400°F/Gas mark 6).

Combine the rice with 500 ml (17 fl oz/2 cups) water in a pan.
Bring to the boil, reduce the heat to low, cover and cook for
15 minutes. Remove from heat, allow to stand covered for
10 minutes.

Heat the oil in a large pan set over high heat. Add the onion
and garlic and cook gently for 2–3 minutes, or until softened.
Add the cream, pasta sauce and semi-dried tomatoes, toss well
to combine.

Line a well-oiled baking dish with cooked rice. Scatter with
tuna, spring onion, basil and diced cheese, season, then pour
over the sauce. Top with grated cheese. Bake for 20 minutes or
until the cheese has melted and browned.

Tuna in Tomato Sauce

1 tablespoon olive oil
4 fresh tuna cutlets

Tomato Sauce
1 onion, chopped
2 garlic cloves, crushed
400 g (14 oz) can peeled
   tomatoes, undrained and
   mashed
125 ml (4 fl oz/½ cup) tomato
   juice
2 tablespoons capers,
   chopped
4 anchovy fillets, chopped
½ teaspoon dried oregano
freshly ground black pepper,
   to taste

Serves 4

Preheat the oven to 180°C (350°F/Gas mark 4).

Heat the oil in a frying pan and cook the tuna for 2–3 minutes on each side. Transfer to an ovenproof dish and reserve the juices.

To make the tomato sauce, cook the onion and garlic in a pan for 4–5 minutes, or until tender. Add the reserved pan juices, tomatoes and juice, capers, anchovies and oregano. Season with black pepper. Bring to the boil and pour over the tuna.

Transfer the tuna and sauce to a baking dish, cover and bake for 20–30 minutes, or until the tuna flakes when tested.

Ricotta-Stuffed Squid

4 small squid hoods, cleaned
2 tablespoons olive oil
1 garlic clove, crushed
400 g (14 oz) can peeled
   tomatoes, undrained and
   mashed
½ teaspoon dried rosemary
60 ml (2 fl oz/¼ cup) dry white
   wine
½ teaspoon sugar
freshly ground black pepper,
   to taste

Cheese Stuffing

45 g (1½ oz) breadcrumbs,
   made from day-old bread
4 tablespoons fresh parsley,
   chopped
115 g (4 oz) ricotta cheese
55 g (2 oz) Parmesan
½ teaspoon dried oregano
1 garlic clove, crushed
pinch of cayenne pepper
1 egg, lightly beaten

Serves 4

To make the cheese stuffing, combine the breadcrumbs, parsley, ricotta cheese, Parmesan, oregano, garlic, cayenne and egg in a bowl. Divide the mixture into four equal portions and spoon into the squid hoods. Secure the ends with a cocktail stick or skewer.

Heat the oil in a frying pan and cook the squid for 3–4 minutes on each side, or until brown. Add the garlic, tomatoes, rosemary, wine, sugar and black pepper. Reduce the heat and simmer for 20–30 minutes, or until the squid is tender.

To serve, remove the skewers, slice the squid and accompany with the sauce.

Spicy Deep-Fried Squid Rings

6 tablespoons plain (all-purpose) flour

2 tablespoons paprika

1 teaspoon salt

450 g (1 lb) fresh squid, cut into rings, or frozen squid rings, defrosted and dried

vegetable oil, for deep-frying

mayonnaise, to serve

Serves 4

Mix together the flour, paprika and salt. Toss the squid rings in the seasoned flour to coat evenly.

Heat 5 cm (2 in) of the vegetable oil in a large heavy pan. Test that the oil is ready by adding a squid ring—it should sizzle at once. Cook a quarter of the rings for 1–2 minutes, until golden. Drain on kitchen paper and keep warm while you cook the remaining rings in 3 more batches. Serve with mayonnaise.

Pan-Fried Squid with Lemon

675 g (1lb 6 oz) squid tubes

85 g (3 oz/½ cup) fine
   semolina

1 teaspoon salt

1 teaspoon freshly ground
   black pepper

250 ml (8 fl oz/1 cup) olive oil

1 lemon, cut into wedges

Serves 4

Cut each squid tube along one side. With a sharp knife, score inside the skin diagonally in both directions, making a diamond pattern. Cut the squid into 2 x 4 cm (¾ x 1½ in) rectangles.

In a bowl, combine the semolina, salt and pepper.

Heat the oil in a large frying pan or wok until hot. Dip the squid into the semolina and cook in batches until lightly brown and crisp. Drain on absorbent paper and serve with lemon wedges.

MEAT and POULTRY

Beef with Mushrooms, and Polenta

50 g (1¾ oz) porcini
  mushrooms, dried
60 ml (2 fl oz/¼ cup) olive oil
6 rump or fillet steaks
1 brown onion, chopped
2 garlic cloves, crushed
310 g (11 oz) button (white)
  mushrooms
60 ml (2 fl oz/¼ cup) red wine
250 ml (8 fl oz/ 1 cup) beef
  stock
2 tablespoons fresh parsley,
  chopped
salt and freshly ground black
  pepper, to taste
extra fresh parsley, chopped
polenta, to serve

Serves 6

Soak the porcini mushrooms in boiling water for 20 minutes. Drain and chop. Set aside.

Heat the oil in a shallow pan, and fry the beef for a few minutes on each side. Remove from the pan. Sauté the onion and garlic for a few minutes, then add all mushrooms and cook over high heat, until they are soft.

Add the wine and stock, bring to the boil, and then simmer, for 10 minutes. Remove from the heat, add the parsley, and season with salt and pepper.

Serve with mushrooms and polenta, and sprinkle with extra chopped parsley.

Tuscan Beef Stew

3 tablespoons olive oil
2 garlic cloves, crushed
1 onion, finely chopped
1½ teaspoons dried rosemary
450 g (1 lb) chuck steak,
    cut into 2–3 cm (¾–1¼ in)
    pieces
¼ teaspoon ground allspice
½ teaspoon ground cinnamon
60 g (2 oz/¼ cup) tomato
    paste
175 ml (6 fl oz/¾ cup) red wine
salt and freshly ground black
    pepper, to taste

Serves 4

Heat the oil in a deep pan. Add the garlic and onion and cook until the onion is translucent. Add the rosemary and cook for 30 seconds.

Add the beef and cook until the meat is brown. Mix in the allspice, cinnamon, tomato paste, red wine, salt and pepper. Cover and cook over a low heat for 1 hour, or until the meat is tender. Remove the pan lid for the last 15 minutes of cooking. Serve hot.

Florentine Pork with Chickpeas

2 tablespoons olive oil

1 onion, finely chopped

1 garlic clove, finely chopped

1 small red chilli, deseeded
and thinly sliced

1 lb (450 g) boneless pork loin
steaks, cut into long thin
strips

4 tablespoons dry white wine

1 teaspoon fennel seeds

400 g (14 oz) can chickpeas,
drained

250g (9 oz) baby spinach

3 tablespoons mascarpone or
double (heavy) cream

salt and freshly ground black
pepper

steamed rice, to serve

Serves 4

Heat the oil in a large frying pan or wok. Fry the onion for
3–4 minutes, until softened, then add the garlic and chilli and
cook for another minute.

Stir in the strips of pork and cook, stirring, over a medium–
high heat for 5 minutes, or until golden and cooked through.
Stir in the wine and fennel seeds and simmer for 3–4 minutes,
stirring.

Add the chickpeas, then the spinach and stir over a high
heat for 3–4 minutes, until the spinach has wilted and any liquid
has evaporated. Stir in the mascarpone or double cream and
season. Serve with steamed rice.

Note: Quick and easy to make, this creamy pork dish gets its
slight aniseed flavour from the fennel.

Chicken with Mushrooms and Sun-Dried Tomatoes

2 tablespoons olive oil

8 chicken pieces (thighs, legs), skin removed

1 onion, chopped

2 garlic cloves, crushed

280 g (10 oz) small button (white) mushrooms

1 teaspoon dried mixed herbs

125 ml (4 fl oz/½ cup) white wine

125 ml (4 fl oz/½ cup) chicken stock

2 tablespoons plain (all-purpose) flour

125 ml (4 fl oz/½ cup) milk

8 large sun-dried tomatoes, sliced

1 tablespoon fresh parsley, chopped

Serves 4–6

Heat the oil in a large, deep frying pan and cook the chicken until browned on all sides. Remove from the pan and set aside.

Add the onion and garlic to the pan and sauté until the onion is translucent. Add the mushrooms and herbs. Cook for 1 minute. Stir in the wine and stock. Bring to the boil.

In a small bowl, mix the flour and a little of the milk together to form a smooth paste. Add the remaining milk and stir into the pan. Cook, stirring, until the sauce boils and thickens.

Return the chicken to the pan and cook for 10–15 minutes. Garnish with sun-dried tomatoes and parsley.

Chicken in White Wine Sauce

2 tablespoons olive oil

55 g (2 oz) butter

6 chicken breast fillets, cut
  into chunks

175 g (6 oz/1 cup) onion,
  chopped

150 g (5 oz/1 cup) celery,
  chopped

150 g (5 oz/1 cup) carrot,
  sliced

450 g (1 lb) tomatoes, peeled

1 tablespoon tomato paste

175 ml (6 fl oz/¾ cup) dry
  white wine

2 whole cloves

pinch of ground cinnamon

2 teaspoons salt

freshly ground black pepper,
  to taste

340 g (12 oz) shell
  (conchigliette) pasta

Serves 6

Preheat the oven to 165°C (320°F/Gas mark 2–3).

Heat the oil and butter in a flameproof casserole dish (use one that has a lid) and brown the chicken evenly all over. Remove the chicken from the dish and set aside.

Add the onion, celery and carrot to the pan and sauté for 5 minutes, stirring occasionally. Add the tomatoes, tomato paste, wine and seasonings. Bring to the boil and mix thoroughly. Replace the chicken in the casserole dish, then cover and cook in the oven for 1 hour, or until the chicken is tender.

Meanwhile, cook the pasta in boiling salted water until *al dente* (about 15 minutes), then drain thoroughly.

To serve, place the pasta in a deep serving dish, arrange the chicken pieces on top and pour over the sauce.

Tuscan Roast Chicken

6–8 chicken pieces (legs and
   thighs), skin removed
60 ml (2 fl oz/¼ cup) olive oil
1 tablespoon dried rosemary
2 garlic cloves, finely chopped

Serves 4–6

Preheat the oven to 190°C (375°F/Gas mark 5).

Place the chicken pieces in a baking dish. Coat the chicken with the oil and sprinkle rosemary and garlic over them.

Bake in the oven for 30 minutes, or until the chicken is cooked. Transfer to a serving dish and serve with roast vegetables.

Liguria Roast Chicken

1 medium chicken
60 g (2 oz/¼ cup) Basil Pesto
   (see recipe page 272)
Parmesan shavings

Serves 4–6

Preheat the oven to 180°C (350°F/Gas mark 4).

Truss the chicken by turning the chicken wings under the chicken back and tying the chicken legs together. Brush the Basil Pesto generously over chicken.

Bake for 1½ hours, or until the juices run clear when tested. Serve immediately, garnished with Parmesan.

Chicken with Porcini Mushrooms

10 g (⅓ oz) dried porcini
  mushrooms
125 ml (4 fl oz/½ cup) boiling
  water
1 tablespoon olive oil
1.5–2 kg (3¼–4 lb) chicken
  pieces, trimmed of fat
2 garlic cloves, crushed
1 onion, finely chopped
280 g (10 oz) button (white)
  mushrooms, sliced
400 g (14 oz) can tomatoes,
  chopped
125 ml (4 fl oz/½ cup) chicken
  stock
400 g (14 oz) baby potatoes,
  washed and halved
4 sprigs thyme and oregano,
  chopped
salt and freshly ground black
  pepper, to taste

Serves 4–6

Place the porcini mushrooms in a small bowl, pour boiling water over, and set aside for 30 minutes. Drain, and reserve the soaking liquid. Chop the mushrooms roughly.

Heat the oil in a pan and add the chicken pieces in two batches. Brown on both sides for a few minutes. Remove the chicken from the pan, and set aside. Add the garlic and onion to the pan, and cook for a few more minutes until soft.

Return the chicken to the pan, add the mushrooms and their liquid, and then add all the other ingredients.

Bring to the boil, reduce the heat, and simmer on a low heat for 40–50 minutes, or until the chicken is tender. Adjust the seasoning before serving.

Duck Ragout with Pappardelle

725 g (1 lb 7½ oz) duck
  breasts
225 g (8 oz) pappardelle
2 tablespoons olive oil
1 onion, diced
2 garlic cloves, crushed
450 g (1 lb) tomatoes, peeled
  and chopped
150 ml (5 fl oz/⅔ cup) veal
  stock
150 g (5 oz) whole black olives
10 fresh sage leaves
salt and freshly ground black
  pepper, to taste

Serves 4

Place the duck breasts in a pan, cover with water, and boil for 5 minutes. Strain the water, and remove the skins from the breasts. Cut into strips, set aside.

Cook the pappardelle in boiling salted water for 15 minutes, or until *al dente*, and set aside.

Heat the oil and sauté the onion and garlic for a few minutes, until the onion is soft. Add the duck pieces and sauté for 1 minute. Add the tomatoes and stock, simmer for 5–10 minutes, until the sauce thickens.

Just before serving, season with salt and pepper, add the olives and sage leaves, and toss through the pappardelle.

Duck with Vinegar

2 tablespoons sunflower oil

4 duck breasts, with skin on

3 tablespoons balsamic
   vinegar

freshly ground black pepper,
   to taste

¼ teaspoon ground cinnamon

4 tablespoons fresh
   blueberries

12 zucchini (courgette) flowers

90 g (3 oz) plain (all-purpose)
   flour

250 ml (8 fl oz/1 cup) water

oil, for cooking

Serves 4

Heat the oil in a frying pan and cook the duck, skin side down, over a low heat until the skin is golden. Turn and cook on the other side.

Add the vinegar, black pepper, cinnamon and blueberries. Cover and cook over a low heat for 15 minutes, or until the duck is tender.

To prepare the courgette flowers, gradually sift the flour into water and mix with a fork until the batter is smooth. If necessary add more water. Pour 2.5 cm (1 in) oil into a frying pan and heat until very hot. Dip the flowers into the batter and cook a few at a time until golden.

To serve, arrange the duck and flowers on a serving plate and spoon blueberry sauce over the duck.

Note: Blueberries are used in this recipe, but any other berry fruit may be substituted.

Lamb Casserole

1 kg (2¼ lb) lamb shoulder
  steaks, diced
500 ml (17 fl oz/2 cups) water
2 carrots, peeled
1 large parsnip, peeled
4 sticks celery, trimmed
2 teaspoons black
  peppercorns
5 bay leaves

Topping

3 eggs
2 tablespoons plain (all-
  purpose) flour
225 g (8 oz/1 cup) natural
  (plain) yogurt
½ teaspoon salt
375 ml (12 fl oz/1½ cups)
  reserved cooking stock

Serves 4–6

Place the meat in a large pan. Add the water and bring to the boil, skimming off the scum that forms on the surface. Add the vegetables, peppercorns and 1 bay leaf to the meat. Cover and simmer for 1½ hours, or until the meat is cooked.

Preheat the oven to 180°C (350°F/Gas mark 4).

Divide the meat into four ovenproof bowls. Strain the cooking liquid, discarding the vegetables and set aside until lukewarm.

To make the topping, lightly beat the eggs. Beat in the flour, yogurt, salt and reserved stock.

Pour the topping over the meat. Place a bay leaf on top of each bowl. Bake for 20 minutes, or until topping is lightly set.

Lamb Cutlets with Olives and Rosemary

1 tablespoon olive oil
2 garlic cloves, crushed
8–12 lamb cutlets, depending
   on size
150 ml (5 fl oz/²/₃ cup) white
   wine
2 tablespoons tomato paste
150 ml (5 fl oz/²/₃ cup) beef
   stock
2 sprigs fresh rosemary,
   roughly chopped
55 g (2 oz) black olives
freshly ground black pepper,
   to taste

Serves 4

Preheat the oven to 180°C (350°F/Gas mark 4).

Heat the oil in a large pan, add the garlic and lamb cutlets, and brown, on medium heat for 2–3 minutes on each side. Add the wine and cook for 2 minutes. Mix the tomato paste with beef stock and add to the lamb cutlets. Add the rosemary, black olives and pepper.

Transfer the lamb to a casserole dish and bake for 30–40 minutes.

Lamb Cutlets with Parmesan and Pesto

1 egg

2 tablespoons Basil Pesto
(see recipe page 272)

2 tablespoons cornflour (corn
starch)

10–12 lamb cutlets

30 g (1 oz/½ cup)
breadcrumbs, toasted

30 g (1 oz/¼ cup) Parmesan
shavings

2 tablespoons olive oil

Serves 4–6

Preheat the oven to 190°C (375°F/Gas mark 5).

Beat the egg, Basil Pesto and cornflour together until combined. Dip the cutlets in the egg mixture and coat. Mix the breadcrumbs with Parmesan. Coat the cutlets with the breadcrumb mixture.

Heat the oil in a roasting pan. Place the cutlets in a pan and turn to coat in the oil.

Bake for 10–15 minutes, turning once during cooking until the cutlets are cooked. Alternatively, shallow-fry the cutlets in oil.

Lamb Shanks with Roast Vegetables

3 tablespoons olive oil

2 parsnips, peeled and cut
   into large chunks

1 medium sweet potato,
   peeled and cut into large
   chunks

1 swede, peeled and cut into
   large chunks

1 bunch spring onions
   (scallions), trimmed

2 garlic cloves, crushed

4 lamb shanks

175 ml (6 fl oz/¾ cup) beef
   stock

60 ml (2 fl oz/¼ cup) water

125 ml (4 fl oz/½ cup) red wine

1 tablespoon tomato paste

2 sprigs fresh rosemary,
   chopped

bouquet garni

salt and freshly ground black
   pepper, to taste

Serves 4

Heat half the oil in a large heavy pan, add the parsnips, sweet potato, swede and onions and cook quickly until brown. Set aside on a plate. Add the remaining oil to the pan and brown the garlic and shanks for a few minutes.

Add the stock, water, red wine, tomato paste, rosemary, bouquet garni, salt and pepper to the pan. Bring to the boil, reduce the heat, and leave to simmer with the lid on for 20 minutes.

Return the vegetables to the pan and cook for another 30 minutes until the vegetables and lamb are cooked.

Before serving, remove the bouquet garni and adjust the seasoning to taste.

Loin of Lamb with Rosemary, Garlic and Sun-Dried Tomatoes

2 x 340–475 g (12–13 oz) lamb
   loins
3 tablespoons olive oil
1 garlic clove, crushed
150 g (5 oz) semi-dried
   tomatoes, sliced
4 sprigs fresh rosemary
freshly ground black pepper
   and salt, to taste

Rosemary Jus
250 ml (8 fl oz/1 cup) beef
   stock
2 teaspoons balsamic vinegar
2 teaspoons sugar
1 tablespoon fresh rosemary,
   chopped

Serves 6

Preheat the oven to 180°C (350°F/Gas mark 4).

Place the lamb on a board, skin-side down, brush the inside with oil, and sprinkle with garlic.

Place half the sun-dried tomatoes and 2 sprigs of rosemary inside each loin of lamb, and season with pepper and salt.

Tie the lamb up with string, place on a roasting rack and roast for 30 minutes, or until the lamb is cooked to your liking. Leave to rest for 10 minutes, covered.

To make the rosemary jus, in a small pan, place the stock, vinegar, sugar and rosemary. Bring to the boil, leave to simmer, and reduce for 5 minutes.

Serve the sliced lamb with the rosemary jus.

Mediterranean Lamb Cutlets with White Bean Medley

1 egg

2 tablespoons cornflour (corn starch)

12 lamb cutlets

30 g (1 oz/½ cup) soft breadcrumbs

2 tablespoons olive oil

White Bean Medley

1 x 400 g (14 oz) can cannellini beans, drained

2 tomatoes, diced

7 g (¼ oz/¼ cup) fresh basil leaves, torn

½ tablespoon balsamic vinegar

1½ tablespoons olive oil

Serves 4

Preheat the oven to 190°C (375°F/Gas mark 5).

Beat the egg and cornflour together. Dip the cutlets into the egg mixture to coat. Coat the cutlets with breadcrumbs, pressing them on.

Heat the oil in a roasting pan. Place the cutlets in a pan, turning to coat. Bake the cutlets for 10 minutes, or until cooked through.

To make the white bean medley, mix the beans, tomatoes, basil, vinegar and oil together.

Serve the cutlets with the white bean medley.

Oven-Roasted Lamb

1 tablespoon olive oil

1–1.5 kg (2–3 lb) lamb, cut into
  chunks

4 potatoes, peeled and diced

4 tomatoes, cut into quarters

2 teaspoons dried oregano

freshly ground black pepper,
  to taste

Serves 4–6

Preheat the oven to 220°C (425°F/Gas mark 7).

   Heat the oil in a roasting pan until very hot. Add the lamb and bake for 5 minutes. Remove the lamb from the pan and set aside. Add the potatoes to the pan, tossing to coat in the pan juices. Bake for 5 minutes. Remove the pan from the oven, return the meat to the pan and add the tomatoes and oregano. Grind the pepper over and toss to coat, taking care not to break up the tomatoes. Bake at 180°C (350°F/Gas mark 4) for 45–50 minutes, or until the meat and potatoes are cooked.

Osso Bucco

30 g (1 oz) butter
1 carrot, peeled and chopped
2 onions, chopped
2 sticks celery, chopped
2 garlic cloves, crushed
4 thick slices shin veal on the
  bone
plain (all-purpose) flour, to
  coat
2 tablespoons olive oil
8 tomatoes, peeled and
  chopped
125 ml (4 fl oz/½ cup) dry
  white wine
250 ml (8 fl oz/1 cup) beef
  stock
1 bay leaf
freshly ground black pepper
1 tablespoon butter mixed
  with 2 tablespoons plain
  (all-purpose) flour

Gremolata
4 tablespoons fresh parsley,
  chopped
1 tablespoon lemon zest,
  finely grated
1 garlic clove, crushed
1 anchovy, finely chopped

Serves 4

Preheat the oven to 180°C (350°F/Gas mark 4).

Melt the butter in a frying pan and cook the carrot, onions, celery and garlic gently for 5 minutes, or until the vegetables are softened. Remove the vegetables from the pan and place in an ovenproof dish.

Coat the veal in the flour. Heat the oil in a frying pan and cook the veal until golden on each side. Remove from the pan and arrange over the vegetables. Add the tomatoes and cook, stirring constantly, for 5 minutes.

Blend in the wine, stock, bay leaf and black pepper, bring to the boil and simmer for 5 minutes. Whisk in the butter mixture and pour over the meat and vegetables. Cover and bake for 1½ hours, or until the meat is tender.

To make the gremolata, combine the parsley, lemon rind, garlic and anchovy. Scatter over the meat just prior to serving.

Polpettone

2 slices white bread, crusts
   removed
60 ml (2 fl oz/¼ cup) milk
450 g (1 lb) pork mince
2 rashers (strips) bacon, rind
   removed and meat diced
2 garlic cloves, crushed
1 egg
¼ teaspoon ground nutmeg
1 teaspoon dried marjoram
2 hard-boiled eggs
3 chipolatas

Serves 4–6

Preheat the oven to 180°C (350°F/Gas mark 4).

Soak the bread in the milk for 5 minutes.

Place the mince, bacon, garlic, egg, nutmeg, marjoram and bread mixture in a bowl. Mix well with your fingertips. Press the mixture out on a lightly floured surface to a 10 x 20 cm (4 x 8 in) rectangle. Place the hard-boiled eggs and chipolatas down the centre of the meat. Roll the meat around the filling. Place in a greased roasting pan and bake for 1 hour, or until cooked. Serve hot.

Note: This is the Italian version of a meatloaf.

Roast Loin of Pork with Mushrooms and Pancetta

2 tablespoons olive oil

1 medium leek, washed and finely sliced

100 g (3½ oz) mushrooms, chopped

50 g (1¾ oz) pancetta, chopped

7 g (¼ oz/¼ cup) fresh parsley, chopped

salt and freshly ground black pepper, to taste

1 kg (2¼ lb) loin of pork

40 g (1⅓ oz) sun-dried tomato paste

250 ml (8 fl oz/1 cup) veal stock

Serves 4–6

Preheat the oven to 180°C (350°F/Gas mark 4).

Heat the oil in a pan, add the leeks, and cook for 3–5 minutes, or until soft. Add the mushrooms, pancetta, parsley, salt and pepper, and cook for another 3 minutes. Set aside to cool.

Cut the pork down the middle and open out. Place the mushroom mixture down the centre of the meat, roll up and tie with string, at 2.5 cm (1 in) intervals.

Rub sun-dried tomato paste over the pork, place on a roasting rack, and bake for 50–60 minutes, or until tender. Cover in foil, and rest for 10 minutes.

Heat the pan juices on the stovetop, and add the veal stock. Scraping the pan with a wooden spoon, bring the stock to the boil, and reduce, for 5 minutes.

Serve with pork in slices with the pan juices.

Saltimbocca

8 thin veal steaks
125 g (4½ oz) ham, thinly
  sliced
½ teaspoon dried sage or
  8 fresh sage leaves
30 g (1 oz) butter
2 tablespoons white wine or
  marsala
2 tablespoons beef stock
½ teaspoon salt
freshly ground black pepper,
  to taste
mushroom risotto, to serve

Serves 4

Place the veal steaks between two sheets of plastic wrap (cling film) and flatten with a rolling pin or the side of a meat mallet. Place a slice of ham, cut to the same size as the veal, on each steak. Place a sage leaf or a light sprinkling of dried sage on top of the ham. Roll up the veal and ham and fasten the rolls with cocktail sticks.

Melt the butter in a frying pan that has a lid and brown rolls on all sides (about 10 minutes). Reduce the heat and add the wine and stock. Add the salt and pepper, stir to lift the pan juices, cover tightly and simmer gently for 20 minutes, turning the rolls occasionally, until the veal is tender and the liquid is reduced to a glaze.

Serve immediately with risotto.

Spatchcock with Rosemary and Lemon

2 x spatchcocks, each 450 g
  (1 lb), halved

Marinade
60 ml (2 fl oz/¼ cup) extra
  virgin olive oil
2 tablespoons lemon juice
1 tablespoon fresh rosemary,
  roughly chopped
1 garlic clove, crushed
freshly ground black pepper,
  to taste

Serves 4

Combine the marinade ingredients in a screw-top jar and shake well.

Place the spatchcocks in a large dish, pour over the marinade, and refrigerate for 3–4 hours.

Preheat the oven to 180°C (350°F/Gas mark 4).

Place the spatchcocks on a roasting rack, and bake for 35–40 minutes, basting every 15 minutes, until cooked.

Veal Parmigiana

4 veal steaks, thinly sliced
2 eggs
2 tablespoons cornflour (corn
　starch)
toasted breadcrumbs, to coat
125 ml (4 fl oz/½ cup) olive oil
150 g (5 oz/1 cup) mozzarella,
　grated (shredded)
4 slices ham off-the-bone
2 tablespoons Parmesan
　shavings

Tomato Sauce
400 g (14 oz) can tomatoes
　and onion
1 red bell pepper (capsicum),
　pith and seeds removed
　and halved
1 tablespoon fresh parsley,
　chopped
1 teaspoon dried basil
1 tablespoon tomato paste
salt and freshly ground black
　pepper, to taste

Serves 4–6

Preheat the oven to 180°C (350°F/Gas mark 4).

On a clean work surface, roll or pound the meat until thin.

Beat the eggs and cornflour together in a bowl. Dip the meat into the egg mixture then coat in breadcrumbs.

Heat the oil in a large frying pan and cook the veal on both sides until golden brown. Drain on paper towels.

To make the tomato sauce, place the tomato and onion in a food processor or blender. Add the capsicum, parsley, basil, tomato paste, salt and pepper and process until smooth.

Place the veal in an ovenproof dish, top with mozzarella, ham, tomato sauce and sprinkle with Parmesan.

Bake in the oven for 15–20 minutes, or until the cheese has melted and is golden.

Veal Scaloppine Marsala

4 very thin veal steaks, cut in
    half
salt and freshly ground black
    pepper, to taste
2 eggs, beaten
3 tablespoons plain (all-
    purpose) flour
45 g (1½ oz) butter
125 ml (4 fl oz/½ cup) dry
    marsala or sherry
125 ml (4 fl oz/½ cup) beef
    stock

Serves 4

Season the veal steaks with salt and pepper. Dip the steaks in egg, then coat lightly with flour and set aside.

Melt half the butter in a frying pan. Add the steaks and brown the meat, for about 5 minutes on each side, taking care not to burn it.

When it is well browned, add half the marsala and swirl the steaks in liquid so that the liquid thickens with the flour and butter. Remove the steaks to warm plates. Repeat with the remaining steak fillets.

Add the stock and remaining butter to the pan. Scrape the base and sides to include all leftover bits in the sauce. Pour sauce over meat and serve.

Quail with Lemon and Sage Leaves

6 tablespoons olive oil

1 tablespoon lemon juice

½ teaspoon lemon zest

1 garlic clove, crushed

salt and freshly ground black
  pepper

4 quails, butterflied

1 bunch sage leaves,
  1 tablespoon chopped; the
  rest to garnish

60 ml (2 fl oz/¼ cup) chicken
  stock

Serves 4

Preheat the oven to 180°C (350°F/Gas mark 4).

Combine 4 tablespoons of olive oil, the lemon juice, lemon zest, garlic, pepper and salt in a bowl. Set aside.

Heat 1 tablespoon of the remaining oil in a large pan, add the quail and chopped sage leaves, and brown quickly. Set aside in a baking dish.

To the pan, add the remaining oil, lemon juice mixture and chicken stock. Return to the heat, bring to the boil, and simmer for 1 minute (to reduce the liquid), stirring with a wooden spoon.

Pour the pan juices over the quail and bake for 20–25 minutes. Garnish with whole sage leaves.

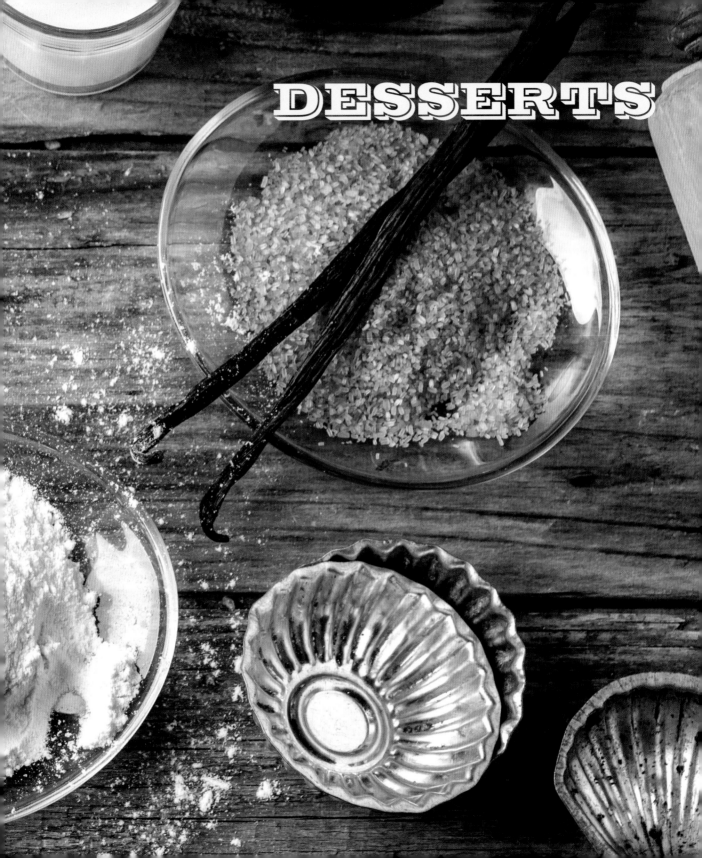

DESSERTS

Honeyed Figs with Mascarpone

12–16 fresh figs, depending
   on their size
2 tablespoons honey
1 tablespoon pine nuts
100 g (3½ oz) mascarpone

Serves 4

Preheat the oven to 180°C (350°F/Gas mark 4).

Cut a deep cross into each fig at the stalk end, then open out slightly. Place the figs close together in an ovenproof dish to keep them upright.

Drizzle the honey over and inside the figs, then cook for 10 minutes, until soft. Meanwhile, place a frying pan over a medium heat and dry-fry the pine nuts for 2 minutes, until golden, stirring often.

Transfer 3–4 figs to each serving plate, scatter the pine nuts around them and serve with a spoonful of mascarpone.

Note: Luscious figs and creamy mascarpone are the perfect end to any meal. Only use ripe fresh figs for this Italian dessert — canned ones are too soft and sweet.

Cassata

20 cm (8 in) sponge cake
60 ml (2 fl oz/¼ cup) almond
   liqueur
chocolate curls, to decorate

Filling

1 litre (1¾ pints) vanilla ice
   cream, softened
250 ml (8 fl oz/1 cup) double
   (heavy) cream
125 g (4½ oz) glacé apricots,
   chopped
125 g (4½ oz) glacé pineapple,
   chopped
60 g (2 oz) glacé cherries,
   chopped
60 g (2 oz) raisins, halved
125 g (4½ oz) dark
   (bittersweet) chocolate,
   grated
125 g (4½ oz) pistachios,
   chopped

Serves 10

To make the filling, place the ice cream, cream, apricots, pineapple, cherries, raisins, chocolate and pistachios in a bowl and mix to combine.

Split the sponge horizontally into three even layers. Place one layer of sponge in the base of a lined 20 cm (8 in) springform tin (pan) and sprinkle with 1 tablespoon of liqueur. Top with one-third of the filling. Repeat the layers to use all the ingredients, ending with a layer of filling. Freeze for 5 hours, or until firm. Remove from the freezer 1 hour before serving and place in the refrigerator.

Just prior to serving, decorate with chocolate curls.

Note: Use the best quality ice cream you can afford. To retain maximum volume and creamy texture, keep the cassata filling mixture chilled until the cassata is assembled.

Almond Macaroons

2 egg whites
115 g (4 oz/½ cup) caster
  (superfine) sugar
140 g (4½ oz) ground almonds
  (almond meal)
¼ teaspoon almond extract
3 tablespoons icing
  (confectioners') sugar

Makes 20

Preheat the oven to 160°C (315°F/Gas mark 2–3).

Beat the egg whites in a grease-free bowl until soft peaks form. Add the sugar a little at a time. Continue beating until the meringue is thick and glossy. Fold the ground almonds, almond extract and 2 tablespoons of icing sugar into the meringue.

Fill a piping bag fitted with a plain nozzle and pipe 4 cm (1½ in) rounds onto a baking tray lined with baking paper. If you don't have a piping bag, use two wet dessertspoons to shape the meringue mixture onto the baking tray. Dust with the remaining icing sugar.

Bake for 25 minutes, or until lightly browned. Cool on the tray. Store in an airtight container.

Fig and Mascarpone Cake

32 sponge fingers
125 ml (4 fl oz/½ cup) marsala
  or sweet sherry
6 fresh figs, sliced
extra figs, to decorate

Mascarpone Custard
3 tablespoons custard
  powder
2 tablespoons caster
  (superfine) sugar
250 ml (8 fl oz/1 cup) milk
250 ml (8 fl oz/1 cup) double
  (heavy) cream
1 teaspoon vanilla extract
340 g (12 oz) mascarpone

Serves 6–8

To make the mascarpone custard, place the custard powder, sugar, milk, cream and vanilla in a pan and whisk until the mixture is smooth. Cook over a low heat, stirring constantly, until the custard thickens. Remove the pan from the heat and set aside to cool.

Fold the mascarpone into the cooled custard and set aside.

Line a 23 cm (9 in) springform cake tin (pan) with baking paper and line the base with half the sponge fingers. Sprinkle with half the marsala, top with half the sliced figs and half the custard. Repeat the layers to use up all the ingredients.

Cover with plastic wrap (cling film) and refrigerate for 4 hours, or until the cake has set.

Remove the cake from the tin. Decorate the top with extra figs. Note: When figs are not in season, fresh strawberries make a suitable substitute for this elegant cake.

Florentines

100 g (3½ oz) butter

115 g (4 oz/½ cup) caster (superfine) sugar

1 tablespoon milk

3 tablespoons plain (all-purpose) flour

60 g (2 oz/¼ cup) mixed fruit peel, finely chopped

60 g (2 oz/½ cup) flaked almonds, roughly chopped

60 g (2 oz/¼ cup) mixed fruit

100 g (3½ oz) dark (bittersweet) chocolate

Makes about 15

Preheat the oven to 180°C (350°F/Gas mark 4).

Put the butter, sugar and milk into a pan. Melt over low heat, stirring constantly until the sugar dissolves. Bring to the boil and cook for 1 minute. Remove from the heat.

Add the flour, mixed peel, flaked almonds and mixed fruit. Place teaspoonsful of the mixture onto a baking tray lined with baking paper, leaving plenty of room for spreading. Flatten slightly.

Bake for 7–10 minutes, or until golden. Leave to cool slightly and reshape if necessary. Transfer to a wire rack.

Melt the chocolate in a bowl set over a pan of gently simmering water. Spread the chocolate over the flat side of the florentines. Make wavy patterns in chocolate and leave to set. Store in an airtight container.

Biscotti Mandorle

300 g (10½ oz) plain (all-purpose) flour

200 g(7 oz/1 cup) caster (superfine) sugar

1 tablespoon aniseed powder

85 g (3 oz) butter, plus extra for greasing

150 g (5 oz) ground almonds (almond meal)

4½ oz (125 g) blanched almonds

30 g (1 oz/¼ cup) pine nuts

2 eggs

4 tablespoons crème de cacao

Makes about 25

Preheat the oven to 170°C (340°F/Gas mark 3½). Lightly grease a baking sheet.

Sieve the flour into a large bowl, add the sugar and aniseed. Rub in the butter until the mixture resembles breadcrumbs.

Stir through the almond meal, blanched almonds and pine nuts.

In another bowl, whisk the eggs with the crème de cacao and add to the other ingredients. Mix until a dough forms, and gently knead to bind all the ingredients.

Divide in half, and form each half into a log 4 cm (1½ in) high and 4 cm (1½ in) wide. Place on the baking sheet, and bake until golden brown, about 30 minutes.

Remove from the oven and allow to cool for 15 minutes. Reduce the oven temperature to 140°C (275°F/Gas mark 1).

Using a serrated knife, cut the logs into 1.5 cm (½ in) slices and return to the baking sheet. Bake for another 50 minutes until crisp.

Passionfruit Zabaglione with Fresh Berries

5 egg yolks

115 g (4 oz/½ cup) caster (superfine) sugar

125 ml (4 fl oz/½ cup) sweet white wine

⅓ cup (2¾ oz) passionfruit pulp

115 g (4 oz) fresh blueberries

150 g (5 oz) fresh raspberries

150 g (5 oz) fresh strawberries

Serves 4–6

Combine the egg yolks and sugar in a heatproof bowl, and beat, until thick and pale.

Add the sweet wine and continue beating. Place the bowl over a pan of simmering water. Continue to beat for 15 minutes, or until the mixture is very thick, not allowing the bowl to overheat too much. The mixture is ready when it forms soft peaks.

Remove the bowl from the heat, and continue beating for another 5 minutes, or until the mixture has cooled. Fold through the passionfruit pulp, and serve with the fresh berries.

For Vanilla Zabaglione, omit the passionfruit pulp and add seeds from 1 vanilla pod (bean) by splitting the pod down the middle and scraping out the seeds.

Tiramisu

1 vanilla pod (bean)

2 eggs, separated

100 g (3½ oz/½ cup) caster (superfine) sugar

250 g (9 oz) cream cheese

250 g (9 oz) mascarpone

250 ml (8 fl oz/1 cup) strong black coffee, cooled

60 ml (2 fl oz/¼ cup) coffee liqueur

22 coffee biscotti fingers

50 g (1¾ oz) milk chocolate, grated

Serves 8

Cut the vanilla pod in half and scrape out the seeds.

Combine the egg yolks, sugar and cream cheese in a mixing bowl. Beat together with an electric beater until light. Add the mascarpone and vanilla seeds and stir to combine.

In a separate bowl, beat the egg whites until soft peaks form. Fold the egg whites into the cream cheese mixture.

Mix the coffee and liqueur together in shallow dish. Dip each biscuit in the coffee mixture.

Place half the fingers in a 12 x 8 in (30 x 20 cm) dish. Spoon over half the cream mixture, top with the remaining fingers and then the remaining cream mixture.

Decorate with grated chocolate. Cover and place in the refrigerator for 2 hours, or overnight.

Lemon Semolina Cake

115 g (4 oz/1 cup) butter

225 g (8 oz/1 cup) granulated (white) sugar

3 eggs

2 teaspoons lemon zest, grated

85 g (3 oz/½ cup) semolina

115 g (4 oz/1 cup) plain (all-purpose) flour

2 teaspoons baking powder

60 ml (2 fl oz/¼ cup) lemon juice

30 g (1 oz/¼ cup) icing (confectioners') sugar

Serves 6–8

Preheat the oven to 180°C (350°F/Gas mark 4).

Melt the butter in a pan large enough to mix all the ingredients. Remove from the heat and mix in the sugar. Add the eggs, lemon zest and semolina. Beat until well combined. Sift the flour and baking powder into the mixture and mix thoroughly.

Pour into a 20 cm (8 in) springform cake tin (pan) lined with baking paper, and bake for 35 minutes.

Mix the lemon juice and icing sugar together in a bowl. Remove the cake from the oven and pour over the lemon juice mixture. Return to the oven and bake for another 10 minutes. Serve warm with whipped cream.

Lemon and Olive Oil Semifreddo

6 egg yolks

175 g (6 oz/¾ cup) granulated
 (white) sugar

125 ml (4 fl oz/½ cup) olive oil

750 ml (1¼ pints/3 cups) milk

250 ml (8 fl oz/1 cup) double
 (heavy) cream

juice of 1 lemon

40 ml (1½ fl oz) limoncello
 liqueur

figs and honey, to serve

Serves 4

In a bowl, beat the egg yolks and sugar until pale in colour and thick in consistency. Slowly blend in the olive oil until combined.

Combine the milk and cream in a large heavy pan and place over medium heat until the mixture starts to simmer. Add a cup of hot milk to the egg mixture, whisking thoroughly, and repeat with the remaining milk.

Return the mixture to the pan and stir quickly over heat for 3 minutes. When the custard starts to thicken, remove from the heat and strain through a fine mesh strainer. Add the lemon juice and the limoncello. Cool to room temperature. Pour into a tray and freeze until solid.

Leave out of the freezer for 10 minutes, slice into pieces and serve with fresh figs and honey.

Lemon Polenta Cake

3 eggs

2 egg whites

250 g (8 oz/1 cup) granulated (white) sugar

2 tablespoons lemon zest, grated

2 tablespoons lemon juice

115 g (4 oz/½ cup) sour cream

150 g (5 oz/1 cup) instant polenta

115 g (2 oz/½ cup) plain (all-purpose) flour

2 teaspoons baking powder

Lemon Sour Cream

225 g (8 oz) sour cream

1 tablespoon lemon zest, grated

1 tablespoon lemon juice

icing (confectioners') sugar, to dust

Serves 6–8

Preheat the oven to 180°C (350°F/Gas mark 4).

Beat the eggs, egg whites and sugar together in a bowl until light and creamy. Fold in the lemon zest, juice, sour cream, polenta, flour and baking powder until just combined.

Pour the mixture into a 20 cm (8 in) springform cake tin (pan) lined with baking paper. Bake for 35 minutes, or until the cake is just cooked.

To make the lemon sour cream, mix the sour cream, lemon rind and juice together.

Serve warm, dusted with icing sugar and with lemon sour cream.

Siena Cake

oil, for greasing

115 g (4 oz/1 cup) blanched almonds, roughly chopped

115 g (4 oz/1 cup) whole hazelnuts

85 g (3 oz/¾ cup) plain (all-purpose) flour

2 tablespoons unsweetened cocoa powder

1 teaspoon ground cinnamon

75 g (2½ oz) dark (bittersweet) chocolate, roughly chopped

85 g (3 oz/½ cup) mixed fruit peel, finely chopped

60 g (2 oz/¼ cup) granulated (white) sugar

150 g (5 oz/½ cup) honey

60 ml (2 fl oz/¼ cup) water

icing (confectioners') sugar, to dust

Serves 10–12

Roast the almonds in a shallow baking tray for 10 minutes, or until lightly coloured. Roast the hazelnuts for 15–18 minutes, or until the skins begin to darken. Remove from the oven and allow to cool slightly. Rub off the skins and chop the nuts.

Preheat the oven to 160°C (325°F/Gas mark 2–3). Grease and line a 20 cm (8 in) springform cake tin with baking paper.

Sift the flour, cocoa and cinnamon into a bowl. Mix in the nuts, chocolate and fruit peel.

Put the sugar, honey and water in a pan. Stir over low heat and bring the mixture to the boil, stirring constantly. Boil without stirring until a soft ball stage. This is when a drop of mixture forms a soft ball in cold water. Mix the sugar mixture into flour and nut mixture until combined. Working quickly, spread into the prepared tin. Smooth the top with the back of a wet spoon.

Bake for 35–40 minutes. Cool in the tin. Dust with icing sugar and serve cut into thin wedges.

Coffee Kisses

225 g (8 oz) butter, at room
   temperature
70 g (2¼ oz) icing
   (confectioners') sugar,
   sifted, plus extra for dusting
2 teaspoons instant coffee
   powder, dissolved in
   1 tablespoon hot water,
   then cooled
225 g (8 oz) plain (all-purpose)
   flour, sifted
3 tablespoons dark
   (bittersweet) chocolate,
   melted

Makes 25

Preheat the oven to 180°C/350°F/Gas mark 4. Line two baking sheets with baking paper.

In a bowl, beat the butter and icing sugar and beat until light and fluffy. Stir in the coffee and flour.

Spoon the mixture into a piping bag fitted with a medium star nozzle and pipe 2 cm (¾ in) rounds of mixture 2 cm (¾ in) apart on the prepared baking sheets.

Bake for 10–12 minutes, or until lightly browned. Leave to set for 5 minutes before turning out onto wire racks to cool completely.

Join the cookies with a little melted chocolate, then dust with icing sugar.

Note: These coffee cookies have a similar texture to shortbread, making the dough perfect for piping. For something different, pipe 5 cm (2 in) lengths instead of rounds. Rather than sandwiching the cookies together with chocolate, you may prefer to leave them plain and simply dust with icing sugar.

Coffee and Ginger Biscotti

Oil, for greasing

115 g (4 oz/1 cup) plain (all-purpose) flour

2 teaspoons ground coffee

3 egg whites

100 g (3½ oz/½ cup) caster (superfine) sugar

75 g (2½ oz) unsalted almonds or hazelnuts

75 g (2½ oz) glacé ginger, finely diced

Makes 40

Preheat the oven to 160°C/325°F/Gas mark 3. Lightly grease a 1 lb (450 g) loaf tin (pan).

Sift together the flour and coffee into a bowl.

In a separate bowl, whisk the egg whites until soft peaks form. Gradually beat in the sugar. Continue beating until the sugar dissolves. Fold in the flour mixture. Fold in the nuts and ginger.

Spoon the batter into the prepared pan. Bake for 35 minutes. Leave to stand on a wire rack until completely cool. When cold, remove the biscotti from the pan. Wrap in aluminium foil. Store in a cool place for 2–3 days.

Preheat the oven to 120°C/250°F/Gas mark ½. Using a very sharp serrated or electric knife, cut the cooked loaf into wafer-thin slices. Arrange on ungreased baking sheets. Bake for 45–60 minutes or until dry and crisp.

Note: You could swap the hazelnuts or almonds and ginger for any whole nut or dried fruit and spice that you prefer. For something festive, try cherries, mixed peel and Brazil nuts, or use pistachios, glacé pears and ground cardamom.

Chocolate Panforte

225 ml (8 fl oz/1 cup) liquid
honey

225 g (8 oz/1 cup) granulated
(white) sugar

250 g (9 oz) almonds, toasted
and chopped

250 g (9 oz) hazelnuts,
toasted and chopped

125 g (4½ oz) glacé apricots,
chopped

125 g (4½ oz) glacé peaches,
chopped

100 g (3½ oz) candied mixed
peel

150 g (5 oz/1¼ cups) all-
purpose (plain) flour, sifted

30 g (1 oz/¼ cup)
unsweetened cocoa
powder, sifted

2 teaspoons ground
cinnamon

165 g (5½ oz) dark
(bittersweet) chocolate,
melted

rice paper

Makes 32

Preheat the oven to 200°C (400°F/Gas mark 6). Line an
18 x 28 cm (7 x 11 in) shallow cake tin with rice paper.

Place the honey and sugar in a small pan and heat, stirring
constantly, over a low heat until the sugar dissolves. Bring to the
boil, then reduce the heat and simmer, stirring constantly, for 5
minutes or until the mixture thickens.

Place the almonds, hazelnuts, apricots, peaches, mixed
peel, flour, cocoa powder and cinnamon in a bowl and mix to
combine. Stir in the honey syrup. Add the chocolate and mix
well to combine.

Pour the mixture into the prepared tin and bake for 20 minutes.
Turn onto a wire rack to cool, then cut into small pieces.

SAUCES, SPREADS and CONDIMENTS

Basic Tomato Sauce

3 tablespoons chopped fresh
   basil
½ teaspoon dried oregano
1½ tablespoons white wine
¼ medium onion, grated
   (shredded)
1 garlic clove, chopped
1 teaspoon olive oil
2 tomatoes peeled, deseeded
   and chopped
1½ teaspoons tomato paste
   (purée)

*Makes 4 fl oz (124 ml/
½ cup)*

In a small bowl, steep (infuse) the basil and oregano in white wine for 10 minutes.

In a frying pan set over medium-high heat, sauté the onion and garlic in olive oil for 5 minutes, stirring frequently. Add the tomatoes and tomato paste, then the herbs and wine. Cover, reduce the heat and simmer for 15 minutes.

Remove the sauce from the heat and purée in a blender or food processor.

Note: The secret to the flavour of this quick, low-fat sauce is steeping the basil and oregano in wine before cooking. This simple step draws out the flavour of the herbs, creating a sauce that tastes as if it has been cooking for hours. This recipe calls for fresh tomatoes, but you may also use canned varieties.

Spicy Pizza Sauce

1 tablespoon olive oil

½ onion, finely chopped

½ red bell pepper (capsicum), chopped

1 garlic clove, chopped

1 teaspoon chilli flakes

1 small red chilli, chopped

14 oz (400 g) can chopped tomatoes

2 tablespoons tomato paste (purée)

1 teaspoon dried oregano

Makes 500 ml (8 fl oz/ 2 cups)

In a pan, heat the oil over medium heat, add the onion, capsicum and garlic. Cook, stirring often until the ingredients are soft.

Mix in the chilli flakes, chilli, tomatoes, tomato paste and oregano. Bring to the boil and cover for about 15 minutes.

Uncover, increase the heat and stir until the sauce thickens and reduces, about 10 minutes.

Garlic-Oregano Pizza Sauce

6 garlic cloves, finely chopped
7 g (¼ oz/ ¼ cup) fresh
  oregano, chopped
125 ml (4 fl oz/½ cup) dry
  white wine
125 ml (4 fl oz/½ cup) olive oil
salt and freshly ground black
  pepper
Parmesan, shavings

Makes 250 ml (8 fl oz/1 cup)

In a small pan over low heat, cook the garlic, wine and half the olive oil until the garlic is very soft, about 30 minutes. The mixture will have the consistency of a rough paste.

Spread the paste on the pizza dough. Drizzle with the remaining olive oil and sprinkle with oregano. Season with salt, pepper and Parmesan.

Basil Pesto

225 g (8 oz/2 cups) fresh basil
  leaves, loosely packed
2 fl oz (50 ml/¼ cup) olive oil
2 tablespoons pine nuts,
  toasted
2 garlic cloves, chopped
½ teaspoon salt
30 g (1 oz) Parmesan, shaved
30 g (1 oz) romano cheese,
  freshly grated (shredded)

Makes 250 ml (8 fl oz/1 cup)

Put the basil, olive oil, pine nuts, garlic and salt in a blender or food processor. Blend or process until smooth.

Transfer to a bowl and stir in the Parmesan and romano cheeses.

Note: The pungent, licorice-like aroma and flavour of basil makes a mouth-watering tomato-less sauce. In the summer, farmers' markets and roadside stands in many areas offer several different varieties of basil that can be used to make an assortment of pestos, each with its own distinctive flavour and colour. You could also substitute fresh spinach for the basil. Pesto also marries well with pasta, rice or even fresh Italian or French bread.

Sun-Dried Tomato Pesto

55 g (2 oz) sun-dried
   tomatoes, drained
2 garlic cloves, roughly
   chopped
55 g (2 oz) capers, drained
1 tablespoon lemon juice
7 g (¼ oz/¼ cup) basil
7 g (¼ oz/¼ cup) Italian
   flat-leaf parsley
75 ml (2½ fl oz/⅓ cup) olive oil
salt and freshly ground black
   pepper, to taste

Makes 175 ml (6 fl oz/
¾ cup)

Place the sun-dried tomatoes, garlic, capers lemon juice, basil
and parsley in a food processor, and process, until the mixture
resembles a paste. Slowly add the olive oil in a steady stream,
until the paste is smooth. Add the salt and pepper, to taste.

Aïoli Italia

3 garlic cloves
salt
1 egg yolk, at room
   temperature
juice of ½ lemon
250 ml (8 fl oz/1 cup) olive oil
white pepper

Makes 300 ml (½ pint)

Place the garlic and 1 teaspoon salt in a food processor, and pulse briefly. Add the egg yolk and lemon juice, and pulse until blended.

Slowly add the oil in a steady stream. Add a pinch of white pepper and adjust the salt to taste.

To thin out the aioli at any stage, add a small dash of water and continue adding the remainder of the oil.

Basil Aïoli

60 g (2 oz) fresh basil leaves
125 ml (4 fl oz/½ cup) olive oil
1 garlic clove, crushed
2 egg yolks
3 teaspoons lemon juice
1 tablespoon water
freshly ground black pepper,
   to taste
salt, to taste

Makes 1½ cups

In a food processor, place the basil, 1 tablespoon oil, garlic, egg yolks and lemon juice. Process until well combined.

With the processor running, add the oil in a thin stream and process, until thick. Add water to make a thinner aïoli. Add salt and pepper.

Balsamic Dressing

60 ml (2 fl oz/¼ cup) olive oil
1 tablespoon balsamic vinegar
½ teaspoon sugar
2 teaspoons sesame oil
salt and freshly ground black
  pepper, to taste

Makes 60 ml (2 fl oz/¼ cup.

Combine all the ingredients in a bowl and whisk until thick. Store in an airtight container in the refrigerator.

Lemon and Garlic Oil

1 lemon
1 large garlic clove
250 ml (8 fl oz/1 cup) olive oil

*Makes 250 ml (8 fl oz/
1 cup)*

Preheat the oven to 120°C (250°F/Gas mark 1).
  Place a clean bottle in the oven for 20 minutes.
  Thinly pare the zest from the lemon, making sure there is no white pith on it. Cut into thin strips.
  Blanch the garlic in boiling water for 3 minutes, then set aside.
  Put the lemon and garlic into the warm bottle. Pour in the olive oil and seal with a stopper. Refrigerate and use within 1 week. This oil is perfect served with salads or crusty bread.

Basil Oil

115 g (4 oz/2 cups) fresh basil,
   washed and dried
1 teaspoon salt
500 ml (17 fl oz/2 cups) olive
   oil

Makes 2½ cups

Place the basil, salt and oil in a food processor or blender and
process until coarsely chopped. Pour into a large hot, clean jar
or bottle. Seal. Refrigerate and use within 1 week.
This oil is perfect with salads or pieces of crusty bread.

Chilli Oil

60 ml (2 fl oz/¼ cup) extra
   virgin olive oil
2 red chillies, seeded and
   finely chopped
1 garlic clove, crushed
2 sprigs fresh rosemary,
   chopped
salt and freshly ground black
   pepper, to taste

Makes ⅓ cup

In a small pan, heat the oil over low heat, turn off the heat, add
the chilli and garlic, and leave for 10 minutes to allow the flavours
to infuse through the oil. Add the rosemary, pepper and salt, and
allow to cool.

Store in an airtight container. Serve on toasted Italian bread as
a starter, or added to pasta dishes for extra flavour.

Herbed Olive Oil Sabayon

4 leaves chervil

4 leaves tarragon

4 leaves parsley

500 ml (17 fl oz/2 cups) dry
  white wine

125 ml (4 fl oz/½ cup) white
  wine vinegar

2 medium shallots, peeled
  and chopped

4 egg yolks

150 ml (5 fl oz/⅔ cup) extra
  virgin olive oil

salt and freshly ground
  pepper

*Makes around 375 ml
(12 fl oz/1½ cups)*

Pick the stems off all of the herbs, Heat a heavy pan and simmer the wine, vinegar, shallots and herb stems together over medium heat to reduce slightly in volume. Strain into a pouring jug and keep warm.

Put the egg yolks in a blender and then, with the blender running, slowly pour in the warm liquid followed by the olive oil. Turn the blender off.

Chop and add the herb leaves and salt and pepper to taste, pulse the blender once or twice, then remove to a warm bowl. Serve warm within 1 hour.

Creamy Aubergine Spread

1 medium eggplant
  (aubergine), halved
  lengthways
3 garlic cloves
2 tablespoons olive oil
2 tablespoons lemon juice
salt and freshly ground black
  pepper, to taste
1 French baguette, thickly
  sliced
fresh basil leaves

Makes about 375 ml
(12 fl oz/1½ cups)

Place the eggplant (skin side up) on a baking tray with the unpeeled garlic and grill (broil) under a hot grill (broiler), until the eggplant skin is black. Turn the garlic frequently and remove from the grill if skin starts to brown. Leave to cool.

Peel away the eggplant skin, drain if necessary, and mash the flesh. Peel the garlic and mash into the eggplant. Add the olive oil, lemon juice, salt and pepper to the eggplant purée. Mix well.

Use to top bruschetta and garnish with basil leaves.

Chickpea and Tomato Spread

400 g (14 oz) can chickpeas,
   rinsed and drained
1 tablespoon Basil Pesto
   (see recipe page 272)
4 medium tomatoes, sliced
salt and freshly ground black
   pepper, to taste
fresh marjoram leaves, to
   garnish
1 French baguette, thickly
   sliced

Place the chickpeas, pesto and salt in a food processor or blender and process until coarsely chopped and mixed.

Pile the chickpea mixture on top of bread slice and top with a tomato slice. Grind over the black pepper and garnish with marjoram leaves.

Index

Published in 2015 by
New Holland Publishers
London • Sydney • Auckland

The Chandlery Unit 009 50 Westminster Bridge Road London SE1 7QY United Kingdom
1/66 Gibbes Street Chatswood NSW 2067 Australia
218 Lake Road Northcote Auckland New Zealand

www.newhollandpublishers.com

A catalogue record of this book is available at the British Library and the National Library of Australia.

ISBN: 9781742576206

Managing Director: Fiona Schultz
Editor: Simona Hill
Design: Lorena Susak
Production Director: Olga Dementiev
Printer: Toppan Leefung Printing Ltd (China)

10 9 8 7 6 5 4 3 2 1

Follow New Holland Publishers on
Facebook: www.facebook.com/NewHollandPublishers